PUBLICATIONS OF THE FACULTY OF ARTS
OF THE UNIVERSITY OF MANCHESTER

No. 13

A TUDOR BOOK
OF RATES

A TUDOR BOOK
OF RATES

edited by

T. S. WILLAN

*Professor of Economic History in the University
of Manchester*

MANCHESTER
UNIVERSITY PRESS

© 1962

Published by the University of Manchester at
THE UNIVERSITY PRESS
316–324, Oxford Road, Manchester 13

Printed in Great Britain by Butler & Tanner Ltd., Frome and London

PREFACE

I AM indebted to the Marquess of Salisbury for permission to obtain a microfilm of the 1562 Book of Rates, and to Miss Clare Talbot, the Librarian at Hatfield House, for facilitating this. The microfilm was kindly supplied by the Folger Shakespeare Library, Washington, D.C. For assistance in dating the 1582 Book of Rates, I am indebted to Mr. I. G. Philip, to the Keeper of Printed Books at the Bodleian Library, Oxford, and to Dr. F. H. Stubbings, the Librarian of Emmanuel College, Cambridge. The identification of some of the items in the 1582 Book of Rates has proved difficult, and in this I wish to thank Professor J. M. Wallace-Hadrill for his helpful suggestions. Finally Dr. N. J. Williams allowed me to draw on his great knowledge of the Elizabethan customs system; I am grateful to him for his advice on some difficult points.

In reprinting the Book of Rates I have retained the spelling and the use of capitals of the original, but have modernized the use of i and j, u and v. I have made no attempt to reproduce the erratic punctuation of the original, which is especially marked in the use of points and commas in the Roman numerals. I have used the form v.xx for five score and v.xx xii (or xij) for five score and twelve (in each case the original has every possible variant). I have made no attempt to collate the Book of 1582 with earlier and later editions. After all, the thing was a working manual and not a sacred text. I have, however, noted variant readings where these helped either in the identification of commodities or in the correction of errors in printing.

T. S. W.

CONTENTS

ABBREVIATIONS

Add. MSS.	Additional Manuscripts (British Museum)
Add. Rolls	Additional Rolls (British Museum)
A.P.C.	*Acts of the Privy Council*
Exch. K.R.	Exchequer, King's Remembrancer
Gras	N. S. B. Gras, *The early English customs system* (Harvard Economic Studies, xviii), Cambridge, Mass., 1918
H.M.C.	*Historical Manuscripts Commission*
Lans. MSS.	Lansdowne Manuscripts (British Museum)
O.E.D.	*Oxford English Dictionary*
Pomet	P. Pomet, *A compleat history of druggs*, 3rd ed., London, 1737
Quincy	J. Quincy, *Pharmacopoeia officinalis et extemporanea: or, A compleat English dispensatory*, London, 1718
Smit	H. J. Smit, *Bronnen tot de Geschiedenis van den Handel met Engeland, Schotland en Ierland, 1485–1585*. Rijks Geschiedkundige Publicatiën, 86, 91. 'S-Gravenhage, 1942, 1950
S.P.	State Papers
S.P.D.	State Papers Domestic

INTRODUCTION

THE administration of the customs during Elizabeth's reign has never been fully investigated or described. It is a complex subject which awaits exploration, as indeed does so much of the administrative history of that period. Some work has been done on the customs as a source of revenue to the Crown, and this has involved a consideration of the efficiency with which the customs service was administered. That in turn has naturally led to some investigation of the extent of smuggling.[1] Indeed in recent years interest seems to have shifted from the study of what the Crown gained in customs revenue to the study of what it lost through the evasion of duties. This may represent a shift of interest from the constitutional problems involved in the Queen's attempt to 'live of her own' during an inflationary period to the administrative problems involved in the running of a bureaucratic customs service. It may, however, simply mean that customs duties are more interesting subjects of study when they are evaded than when they are paid. The payment of duties has certainly none of the attraction which marks their evasion. Whether evaded or paid, such duties need fuller study than they have hitherto been given by either the historians of smuggling or the historians of the public revenue. In a sense they need looking at through the eyes of a nineteenth-century free trader or of a twentieth-century protectionist, either of whom would want to know whether the duties were high or low, whether they took account of

---

[1] The best studies of smuggling during this period are G. D. Ramsay, *English overseas trade during the centuries of emergence*, ch. vi, and N. Williams, *Contraband cargoes*, ch. 2.

changing prices, and whether they were protectionist or not. It is with these points in mind that the Elizabethan customs duties will be briefly examined.

Those duties were levied on both exports and imports but not, of course, on goods shipped coastwise. In theory almost all goods entering into foreign trade were subject to duty. There were, however, some exceptions. No duties were levied on ships' stores or, apparently, on small quantities of goods imported for the owner's personal use. Thus in 1552 a Commission on the King's courts of revenue reported that 'divers merchants and other oftentimes make request to the customer for divers and sundry things that is close packed for their store and for their occupying which they may have without paying of custom'. It was not suggested that this practice should cease, but that order should be taken 'that all such things be seen by the officers or by such as shall be appointed either at the waterside or otherwise for therein is suspected to be much deceit used'.[1] Whether or not deceit was used, the duty-free allowance for 'store or provision' was certainly made to cover a wide variety of imported goods. In a London Port Book of Michaelmas 1574 to Easter 1575 the Collector of tonnage and poundage recorded the goods imported 'for store or provision', upon which no duty was paid. They included household goods, some of which were imported by alien immigrants, linen cloth and flax, Danzig chests and Venice carpets, cabbages and cherry trees, writing desks and 'sowinge deskes', three cases 'of pictures of the x commandementes' and two cases containing 'xxvj pectures of mens faces', and 'j tonne rasens', which seems a liberal allowance. They also included one 'fat' of books 'for the Scotish kinge', who was then eight years old.[2]

In addition to these allowances for 'store or provision',

[1] Add. MSS., 30198, f. 42v.   [2] Exch. K.R. Port Books, 6/3.

there were a few other exemptions from the payment of duty.
The Queen did not pay duties to herself for goods imported
on behalf of the Crown; such goods were chiefly arms and
munitions. Similarly no duties were paid on the costly
presents sent to or received from foreign rulers, and no doubt
English ambassadors, returning with the spoils of diplomacy,
enjoyed a like immunity. Finally there was bullion. Its
export was forbidden and its import encouraged. When exported under licence or when imported, bullion paid no
duty. This immunity can only be deplored by the student
of the 'price revolution', for it makes the movement of
the precious metals difficult to trace and impossible to
assess.

Despite the 'free list', it is clear that most goods were
dutiable, whether exported or imported by native or alien
merchants. The alien merchant paid higher duties than the
native. On most goods he paid 25 per cent more than did the
native merchant. On some goods, however, the difference
was much greater than this: on exported woollen cloth the
alien paid a duty more than double that paid by the native.
Here indeed, in the case of woollen cloth, the old threefold
division into native, Hansard, and alien precariously survived into Elizabeth's reign, with different duties for each
category of exporter. Though for a time the Hansard continued to pay less duty on his cloth than other aliens did, he
no longer paid less than native merchants, as once he had
done. Nor was he able for long to maintain his advantage
over other aliens. The real division was now between native
and alien, with the latter including the Hansards. It is with
the former, with the native merchant and the duties he paid,
that this sketch is mainly concerned.

Basically, customs duties can be divided into two different
types. They can consist either of specific or of ad valorem

duties. Specific duties, as their name implies, involve the payment of a certain or specific sum on a given quantity of a commodity. Thus a certain sum was payable as duty on a sack of wool, on a tun of wine, and on a short cloth. The ad valorem duties, again as their name implies, were assessed on the value of goods; they consisted of a certain percentage of that value. Both types of duty were used during Elizabeth's reign, though in fact most goods, especially those imported, were subject to ad valorem and not to specific duties. Specific duties were levied on a very narrow range of exports and imports, but within that range were some of the most important commodities entering into English foreign trade. It may be well, therefore, to examine the specific duties first.

1. SPECIFIC DUTIES

There were three specific duties of great importance in the Elizabethan tariff system. They were the import duty on wine and the export duties on wool and on woollen cloth.

In value wine was probably the most important article that was imported into Elizabethan England. The wine was of many sorts and was subject to a complicated system of duties which cannot be fully investigated here. The basic duty, the tonnage of the Tonnage and Poundage Act, was 3s. a tun, but even this did not apply to all wines. Rhenish wine was to pay 1s. an aam as tonnage.[1] These were low duties, but they were only the beginning. Rhenish wine paid in addition an ad valorem duty of 1s. in the £ on its value, which was put at 10s. an aam.[2] French wines, the most

---

[1] 1 Eliz., c. 20. The aam was apparently 40 gallons.
[2] Infra, p. 64.

important of all, were subject to an imposition of 50s. 4d. a tun, which, with the 3s. tonnage, made 53s. 4d. in all.[1] It is difficult to translate this figure into ad valorem terms, for the sort of prices upon which such a calculation could be based are largely lacking. Early in Elizabeth's reign French wine seems to have been sold at about £6 a tun, which included the duty.[2] In that case the duty amounted to some 80 per cent ad valorem. The duty on sweet wines was lower than that on French wines, but it was still fairly heavy, especially after the levying of a new imposition in 1573. Without going further into the complexities of the wine duties, which would involve a consideration of prisage as well, it is clear that such duties were generally heavy. The successful smuggling of wine would obviously be a profitable occupation.

The duty on exported wool was heavy too.[3] In 1558 it amounted to 40s. a sack for native merchants,[4] which was equal to an ad valorem duty of some 25 per cent. Moreover the loss of Calais, which had been the headquarters of the Staplers Company, forced that Company to seek a staple elsewhere. It began shipping wool to Bruges, but it was only allowed to do so on payment of an additional duty of a mark (13s. 4d.) a sack. In 1560 this additional duty was

---

[1] The imposition on French wine seems in theory to have been 53s. 4d. (A.P.C. 1558-70, p. 102), but in practice to have been levied at that rate only on alien merchants. Native merchants apparently paid 50s. 4d. (Smit, ii. 1065; E. A. Lewis, *The Welsh Port Books (1550–1603)*, pp. 325-6; F. C. Dietz, *English public finance, 1558 1641*, p. 307).

[2] Some wine prices are collected together in A. L. Simon, *The history of the wine trade in England*, ii. 283–91.

[3] The specific duties on exported woolfells and leather were also high. Woolfells (sheepskins with the fleece on them) paid a duty of 40s. for 240 fells in 1558; the duty on woolfells had obviously to be related directly to the duty on wool. The duty on exported leather was £4 a last, but the export of leather was forbidden by statute (1 Eliz., c. 10); some leather was, however, exported under licence.

[4] Technically the 40s. was made up of custom 6s. 8d., subsidy 33s. 4d.

raised to two marks or 26s. 8d. Finally, in May 1561, the
Company received a new charter, and then the duty was
fixed at £3 a sack for the first 3000 sacks exported; exports
above 3000 sacks were to pay a duty of 53s. 4d. a sack. In
practice exports seem rarely, if ever, to have exceeded 3000
sacks p.a.[1] Thus wool was burdened with an export duty of
£3 a sack, equal to some 37 per cent ad valorem. Such a
duty was plainly heavy and likely to encourage smuggling,
especially as much, but not all, of the wool exports were
monopolized by members of the Staplers Company. That
Company was linked to a dying trade, for the export of wool
had fallen to a negligible amount by the fifteen-seventies.
How far that decline was due to the heavy duties on wool,
and how far the legitimate wool exports had been replaced
by smuggling, it is impossible to say.

The duty on exported cloth was more important, for cloth
was the chief export of the period, accounting perhaps for
three-quarters of the total exports by value. The specific duty
on exported cloth applied to woollen broadcloth, the so-
called cloth of assize. Down to 1558 this duty had been
very small, only 1s. 2d. for a short cloth exported by a native
merchant. In 1558 this duty was raised to 6s. 8d. a short
cloth. This new duty was not based at all on the value of the
cloth, but on the amount of wool in a cloth and the duty
that wool would have paid had it been exported as wool and
not as cloth. It was calculated that a sack of wool, which paid
40s. in duty, made four short cloths. Therefore a short cloth
should pay 10s. duty, but 'upon divers considerations at this
time (us and our councel mooving)' the Queen was 'pleased
to assesse' the duty at 6s. 8d. Thus the short cloth paid 6s. 8d.,
and other cloths were related to this basic unit: three kerseys

[1] E. E. Rich, *The ordinance book of the Merchants of the Staple*, pp. 11, 22–3,
30, 35.

or two northern dozens were reckoned as equal to one short cloth, and so on.[1]

It is very difficult to translate this specific duty into ad valorem terms. In practice the duty was applied to a wide range of cloth, differing greatly in quality and value. It applied equally to undyed, undressed cloth and to cloth fully dyed and dressed.[2] A study of the surviving 'cloth books' among the Port Books shows this clearly. There the unfinished cloth exported by Merchant Adventurers was recorded side by side with the finished Suffolk cloths sent to Russia and to Morocco. In either case the duty was 6s. 8d. a short cloth.[3] Even within the broad divisions of unfinished and finished cloth, there must have been considerable differences of quality and value. It is not possible to determine values over the whole range of cloth of assize; it is only possible to give some examples of wholesale prices and of valuations which can be used to convert the 6s. 8d. duty into its ad valorem equivalent. For this purpose the standard histories of prices are of little use. They do not give the price which the merchant paid for cloth he exported, and it is that price which is needed for the calculation of the duty in percentage terms.

Some such prices can be ascertained. In 1564, for example, a London merchant exported 140 Suffolk and Kentish cloths to Morocco. They cost him £1220, and the duty payable would be about 3·4 per cent of that.[4] Two years later,

[1] Infra, pp. 23–4. It is sometimes said that cloth exports were also subject to an ad valorem duty of 3d. in the £, but there seems to be no evidence that such a duty was levied on the cloth exported by native merchants.

[2] The 'Rates for clothes' (infra, p. 74) include a duty of 2d. yard on cloth in grain and 1d. yard for cloth in half grain, but there does not seem to be any evidence that this duty was in practice levied on either native or alien merchants.

[3] Exch. K.R. Port Books, 2/1.

[4] T. S. Willan, *Studies in Elizabethan foreign trade*, pp. 121–2.

Thomas Laurence, a Merchant Adventurer, was buying Devonshire kerseys at prices ranging from 33s. to 48s. each. On the cheaper cloth the duty works out at 5 per cent, on the dearer at 4 per cent. The long Worcester cloths, which Laurence bought in November 1566, cost from £9 to £16 apiece. The duty he would pay ranged from 5 to 2·8 per cent ad valorem.[1] Rather fuller information is available from a very incomplete list of exports for 1570. This list gives various sorts of cloth together with their values. On the more important types of cloth the duty of 6s. 8d. a short cloth works out as follows in ad valorem terms: Wiltshire cloth 6·66 per cent, Kentish cloth 4·2 per cent, Suffolk cloth 6·6 per cent, Gloucestershire cloth 6·5 per cent, Hampshire kerseys 6·1 per cent, and Devonshire kerseys 5·5 per cent.[2]

Finally, a more concrete example of the payment of the cloth duty can be given. In the fifteen-eighties a partnership, which included the Earl of Leicester, was formed for trading with Morocco.[3] The partnership's accounts show that 41 short and 10 long cloths were bought in 1585 at prices ranging from £5 to £10 a cloth; the total cost was £369 13s. 4d. The cloths were exported to Morocco; they were reckoned as equivalent to 54 short cloths (and not 54⅓ which was

[1] Exch. K.R. Accounts, Various, 520/24. Although all kerseys were supposed to pay duty at the rate of 3 kerseys to a short cloth, it is clear that Devonshire kerseys were ranked with Devonshire dozens at 4 to a short cloth (Cotton MSS., Titus B IV, f. 225; Smit, ii. 916).

[2] Cotton MSS., Titus B IV, f. 225. Printed in H. Hall, *A history of the custom-revenue in England*, ii. 243–4. Hall's version is misleading in one respect; he does not make it clear that the number of cloths in his second column (headed 'Bulk') sometimes represents, not the actual number of the cloths, but that number converted into short cloths according to the ratio used for the assessment of duty. Thus he gives 'Hants. kerseys 503⅓', but the MS. has 1510 Hants. kerseys (which at 3 kerseys to a short cloth equalled 503⅓ short cloths).

[3] For this partnership see T. S. Willan, *Studies in Elizabethan foreign trade*, pp. 240–65.

their strict equivalent)[1] and therefore paid duty of £18 or
4·86 per cent of their cost. Two years later the partners
shipped to Morocco 20 broadcloths which had cost £6
apiece; they paid duty on 18 at 6s. 8d. a cloth, which came to
exactly 5 per cent of their cost.[2] In this case one cloth in
ten had been allowed duty free as a wrapper; this was a
customary allowance, but the earlier Moroccan example,
where only ⅓ of a cloth did not pay duty, suggests that it was
not universal. When the allowance was granted, it had the
effect of reducing the duty from 6s. 8d. to 6s. a short cloth.
Some of the percentages which have been given here should
perhaps be slightly reduced to take account of this allowance.

It is in the nature of fixed specific duties, based as they are
on quantity rather than price, that they become in effect
lighter as prices rise. Prices rose during Elizabeth's reign,
and it seems certain that wine, wool, and cloth shared in that
rise. Hence the duties on imported wine and on exported
wool and cloth came to represent a smaller and smaller percentage of the value of these commodities. Even so, the
wine and wool duties remained high. That was not true of
the duties on exported cloth; they had never been high, at
least for native merchants. In the early part of the reign they
seem to have been equivalent to 5 or 6 per cent ad valorem.
If the price of cloth rose, these percentages must have fallen.
Even if the price of cloth did not rise, the duties remained
low, though they fell more heavily on the cheaper cloth than
on the more expensive.[3] Duties which work out at 5 or 6 per

[1] One long cloth was counted as 1⅓ short cloths.
[2] Evelyn MSS., 155, ff. 9, 90 (Christ Church Library, Oxford).
[3] This is clear from the Isham accounts (Northamptonshire Record
Office). In the fifteen-sixties John Isham was paying £40 to £42 for a pack
of ten short cloths; on these the duty would be 8 per cent ad valorem.
Similarly on 651 kerseys, bought for £881, the duty works out at 8 per cent,
but on checked Halifax kerseys, which cost 10s. to 13s. 4d. each and which

B

cent ad valorem seem too low to attract the smuggler, but some cloth was certainly smuggled out of the country.[1] Such smuggling may have been an attempt to evade not only the export duty but also the need for a licence. The export of unfinished white cloth worth more than £4 a cloth and of unfinished coloured cloth worth more than £3 a cloth was forbidden by statute.[2] This prohibition must have covered most of the cloth suitable for export, since the main continental markets would only take unfinished cloth. In practice the prohibition was nullified by the grant of export licences for unfinished cloth. Such licences had to be paid for, though the Merchant Adventurers Company had a free licence for the export of 30,000 cloths p.a. The smuggler would avoid both the cost of the licence and the cost of the duty, but it is doubtful whether the two together amounted to more than 8 or 9 per cent of the value of the cloth. Whether such a charge was high enough to stimulate large-scale smuggling, it is difficult to say. At least, it was fortunate that the products of the cloth industry were not more heavily burdened when they sought a 'vent' abroad. Wine was a luxury, and wool could be used at home, but an export market for cloth was essential if the country's chief industry was to be sustained. To some degree the main specific duties reflect this state of affairs.

2. AD VALOREM DUTIES

Most imports and many exports paid an ad valorem and not a specific duty; they paid a duty of 1s. in the £, or in

were probably rated at 4 to a short cloth, the duty amounts to as much as 16⅔ per cent. I am indebted for this information to Dr. G. D. Ramsay, who is editing the Isham accounts.

[1] N. J. Williams, 'Francis Shaxton and the Elizabethan Port Books', *English Historical Review*, lxvi. 387–95.
[2] 27 Henry VIII, c. 13.

other words a duty amounting to 5 per cent of their value.
This was the poundage as laid down in the Tonnage and
Poundage Acts.[1] Such a duty implies that goods have a
definite value known both to merchants and to customs
officers, and that this value will be the basis on which the
duty is assessed. The duty in fact will be 1s. in the £ or
5 per cent of that value. In practice a list of goods exported
or imported was drawn up; each of the goods was given a
definite value, and the duty was assessed on that value. Such
lists have become known as Books of Rates. This title is a
conventional one and it is rather misleading. It is conventional because the Elizabethan Books actually bear the title
The Rates of the Custom House. It is misleading because the
Books do not really record rates, but values; they are concerned less with the rates of duty than with the value of
goods upon which the duties were based. Nevertheless it is
convenient to retain the conventional title, especially as
contemporaries used 'rate' in the same sense as the later
'official value'.

The origin of the Books of Rates is very obscure.[2] Two
centuries ago Sir Geoffrey Gilbert pointed out that 'a
pound rate could hardly be well and equally assest without a
Book of Rates; since, without such a Book, the customs
would be liable either to the oath of the merchant, or the
oppression of the officer'. He believed that such Books went
back to 1303 when 'the merchants agreed to be charged with
the pound rate according to value'.[3] The institution of ad
valorem duties must have made necessary some sort of

[1] E.g. 1 Eliz., c. 20. Alien merchants paid an additional poundage of 3d.
in the £.
[2] This question has been investigated by N. S. B. Gras in his article
'Tudor "Books of Rates": a chapter in the history of the English customs',
Quarterly Journal of Economics, xxvi (1911–12), 766–75, and in his book *The
early English customs system* (1918), 121–9.
[3] Sir Geoffrey Gilbert, *A treatise on the Court of Exchequer* (1758), pp. 223–4.

valuation of goods for customs purposes, but no actual Book of Rates seems to have survived for the medieval period. The earliest list of goods and their values, which may have been used for the assessment of duties, seems to date from the end of the fifteenth century. The list is headed 'Spycery', but it includes cloth, metals, and other goods as well as spices. It is a curious list, without alphabetical order and without any value ascribed to many of the items.[1] Gras suggested that it was a primitive Book of Rates applying to London only.[2] That may be so, but it is not certain that the list was intended for the assessment of customs duties. It may indeed have had some connection with the activities of the Grocers Company, but that cannot be proved.[3]

Whatever the purpose of this early list of 'Spycery', there is no doubt that a list of goods with their values, drawn up on 15 July 1507, was a Book of Rates.[4] It was described as 'A rate made of the prisys of allmaner off warys' by the King's Council and by the advice of the surveyors, controllers, and customers of London 'and the marchants adventerers of the same'. This Book of Rates does not seem to have been issued as a printed book, and indeed it only survives in an eighteenth-century transcript. It does not distinguish between exports and imports, but it does arrange the goods in rough alphabetical order. Though the Book names some 300 separate commodities, to which 15 have no value attached to them, it obviously did not include quite all the goods exported or imported at that time. There is no reference to alum or cables or lead, for example.

The Book of Rates of 1507 was probably intended for use

[1] R. Arnold, *The customs of London*, pp. 234–7.
[2] Gras, p. 123.
[3] It is rather suggested by the 'Item for rekening for grocery ware' at the end of the list, which includes 'rebate for tare' and 'rebate for trete'.
[4] Printed in Gras, pp. 694–706.

in London and not throughout the country. It was reissued in 1532, again almost certainly only for use in London.[1] Some valuation of goods must have been used in the provincial ports, and the evidence rather suggests that such ports used the same valuations as those in the Book of Rates, at least for some goods.[2] There was, however, no uniform system of valuation before 1536. In that year an 'ordinance devised for thadvancement of the custome' declared that there was no one general valuation of goods that applied throughout the realm. On the contrary, none of the valuations in any of the ports agreed 'one with another'. Therefore the King and his Council, with the advice of the Merchant Adventurers and of the officers of the customs, decreed that there should be one general rate or valuation to serve throughout the realm. This was to be embodied in a Book of Rates which was 'to be comyttyd and delyvered to the officers of the custom and subseedy of every porte'.[3] This Book of Rates does not seem to have survived, but the application of valuations on a national basis was a significant move in the achievement of administrative uniformity. It was a necessary step in the creation of a national customs system, and reflected the growing tendency to regard the country as an economic and administrative unit.

Though Gras emphasized the importance of the decree of 1536 in establishing a national system of valuations for imports and exports, he did not make it clear that this was to be combined with a revaluation which would take account of the rise in prices since 1507.[4] Yet this was clearly the intention. It was said that 'a trew and a just value' was to be

---

[1] Ibid., pp. 124, 705.
[2] Some at least of the valuations used in the east-coast ports are the same as those in the 1507 Book of Rates (Smit, i. 160-9, 190-208, 218-20, 260-4, 276-82).
[3] S.P. Henry VIII, cxiii, ff. 129-40.   [4] Gras, p. 124.

assigned to all goods brought into or carried out of the realm, because 'wares be of a highar value now by the one half and more thein they were in tymes past, so that the Kyng is not nowe answaryd vjd. of the pownd'.[1] Though the rates of 1536 are not known, it seems clear that no revaluation took place then. All the evidence suggests that the rates of 1507 were retained, and that it was those rates which were extended to the whole country in 1536.

The failure to effect a revaluation in 1536 is shown by the first printed Book of Rates, which was issued in 1545.[2] This separated the imports from the exports, listing the former in a rough alphabetical order; the exports, which included a few re-exports, were not arranged alphabetically. The Book also gave some miscellaneous information on weights and measures, on the merchandise of Prussia, Ireland, and 'Iseland', on the 'rewle of ostelage in Spayne', and on the 'rewle of saynt Georges Chappell at saynt Lucas in Spayne'. Where they can be compared, the valuations of goods imported and exported were, with very few exceptions, the same as those of 1507. There were some differences, which may be due to mistakes made either in the 1507 or in the 1545 Book of Rates. Thus jet was valued at 20s. the barrel in 1507 and at 40s. in 1545; 'marmelado' was valued at £4 the lb. in 1507, which was clearly an error, and at 4d. the lb. in 1545. In one important respect the Book of 1545 did differ from its predecessor of 1507; it gave the values of some 790 items, compared with about 300 in 1507. It is impossible to tell how this increase had come about; whether it was of gradual growth over the years, or whether it represented some large inclusion of new items in 1536 or 1545. Nor is it easy to tell

---

[1] S.P. Henry VIII, cxiii, f. 130v.

[2] *The rates of the custome house bothe inwarde and outwarde the dyfference of measures and weyghts and other commodities very necessarye for all marchantes to knowe newly correctyd and imprynted.* London, 1545 (Bodleian 8° C 23 Jur.).

whether the valuations of these new items bore any closer
relation to current prices than did the valuations of the old
items which had remained unchanged since 1507. It is clear
that no general revaluation had taken place by 1545. Nor had
it done so five years later. A Book of Rates for 1550, which
has only survived in an imperfect form, merely repeats the
valuations of 1545.[1]

By the middle of the sixteenth century the Book of Rates
had developed into a printed handbook which listed the
official valuations given to imports and exports. It had
separated the imports from the exports, and had listed the
former in a very rough alphabetical order. That order was so
imperfect as to give the impression that sixteenth-century
Englishmen had as much difficulty with their alphabet as
with their arithmetic. Perhaps the evolution of a strict
alphabetical order should be added to the transition from
Roman to Arabic numerals as a factor in the development of
modern capitalism. Though the form of the Book of Rates
had developed, the valuations themselves had remained
curiously static. With increased inflation this meant that the
valuations bore less and less relation to prices. This was
recognized in the fifteen-fifties as it had been twenty years
earlier. In 1552 the Commission on the King's courts of
revenue drew attention to the matter in that part of their
'certificate' which was headed 'Remembrance of things
touching the Kings Customs'.[2]

The commissioners stressed 'that the Rates should be new
made were very necessary for the Kings highnese profitt and

---

[1] *The rates of the custome house bothe inwarde and outward, the differen[ce] of
measures and weyghtes and [o]ther commodities, very necessarye for all merchauntes
to knowe, newely corrected and imprynted*. London, 1550. The only copy of this
edition is in Cambridge University Library. It is very imperfect, consisting
only of the pages giving the imports under A, B, C, and part of D.
[2] Add. MSS., 30198, ff. 43–43v.

for ease of the merchants, for many kinds of wares be at the discretion of the Customers and Collectors and many kinds of wares be greatly advanced in their prices'. They supported their last statement by giving some examples of increased prices, though with considerable exaggeration. Thus a tun of oil was rated at £4 and was 'of the value of' £30; a ton of iron, rated at £2, was of the value of £26. In all, 14 items were given; their total rating was £27 18s. 8d. and their total value £113 17s. to £114 17s.[1] Eight of the items had appeared in the 1507 Book of Rates,[2] and the rating given to them was the same as in that Book. This is hardly surprising, for the commissioners explained that 'the Book of Rates in the custom house whereby the King is paid custom by the name of poundage . . . was made the xvth day of July in the xxij^{d} year of King Henry VII'. Since that time wares had 'much encreased in value' and 'many kind of wares there be now brought into the realm which then were not made, which pay custom by discretion of the Customer'. For all these reasons it was 'very meet to take order that the Book of Rates be new made in such reasonable sort as may be indifferent for the King and favourable to the merchant, and therein the Kings Majestie shall much advantage the profitt of this custom, specially inwards, and be more certainly answered then he is now'. These were valid reasons for revising the Book of Rates, but they had no immediate effect. It was not a propitious time for recommending reforms; the commissioners had reported on 12 December 1552, and a little over six months later, Edward, whose revenue might have benefited from reform, was dead.

[1] The full list is in Gras, p. 128 n. 6. Sarsenet of Florence was said to be worth £8 to £9, which accounts for the £1 difference in the total values.
[2] Gras, p. 128 n. 6, gives only 7 items as having the valuations of 1507, but 'velvets out of grain' of 1552 was presumably the same as the 'velvettes of all manner colors save ryght crymson' of 1507.

It was left for Edward's sister to take up the project of reforming the Book of Rates, but neither Mary nor her ministers showed any eagerness for the task. No doubt there were more pressing problems during the earlier part of Mary's reign, and it was not until 1558 that a new and revised Book of Rates was produced. The fact that the issue of a new Book followed close on the loss of Calais led earlier scholars to believe that the two events were connected. They thought that the loss of Calais brought 'the Calais duties' to an end, and so it was 'very necessary to increase the Rates' to compensate for this.[1] There was, as Gras pointed out,[2] no truth in this view; no additional revenue had been raised from duties levied at Calais, and the fall of the town brought financial gain, not loss. Indeed the reason for issuing a new Book of Rates in 1558 must be sought, not in any external events, but in the unsatisfactory state of the existing system of valuations for customs purposes. The old Book of Rates was out of date. It did not include many goods which entered into foreign trade. The goods it did include were assigned values which bore no relation to prices; many of these values had been fixed in 1507, and the rise in prices in the interval had made them more and more unreal. Moreover it was not only the valuations for levying ad valorem duties that required revision, it was also the specific duty on cloth. The low specific duty on exported cloth dated from the time when wool, not cloth, was the chief export. That time was past, as the boom in cloth exports of the early fifteen-fifties had served to emphasize.[3] Thus the great shift in the export trade from wool, which paid a high duty, to cloth, which

[1] Sir Geoffrey Gilbert, *A treatise on the Court of Exchequer*, p. 225.
[2] Gras, pp. 127–8.
[3] For the figures of cloth exports from London see F. J. Fisher, 'Commercial trends and policy in sixteenth-century England', *Economic History Review*, x. 96.

paid a low duty, made it necessary to increase the specific duty on cloth if the Crown were to benefit financially from this change in trade. It is true that the cloth duties could have been increased without any general revision of the Book of Rates, for the 1545 Book makes no mention of such duties, but it is significant that the new Book of 1558 gives an account of the increased cloth duties and of the reasons for imposing them.

3. THE REVISED BOOK OF 1558

The revised Book of Rates was issued on 28 May 1558. It was explained to the customs officers that the subsidy of tonnage and poundage was granted by Act of Parliament and that the proceeds were used for the defence of the realm. As it was reasonable that the Crown should be duly answered of the said subsidy, it had caused 'the pryses and values' of all goods liable to the payment 'of the saide subsidie or pondage' to be examined. By the advice of the Council, the Crown had caused the goods 'with theire reasonable and indiferente values and prises . . . to be particulerlie entred and expressed in this presente booke conteynenge in leaves wrytten on bothe sydes twentie and sixe'. The customers were to use the Book and the rates in it; to enable them to do this, 'a parfytte duplicamente of this booke' was to be sent to every port to remain in the custom house there. It would appear that the Books sent to the ports were in manuscript, for no printed copy of them seems to have survived. The Book of Rates itself survives through its enrolment on the Patent Rolls on 28 May 1558.[1]

The Book of 1558, as enrolled on the Patent Rolls, in-

---

[1] Patent Rolls, 4 and 5 Philip and Mary, pt. 3, ms. 12d–22d. There is a modern transcript of the Book in the Round Room at the P.R.O. Add. MSS., 25097, appears to be an imperfect copy of the 1558 Book of Rates.

cluded the order to the Lord Chancellor for the enrolment
in Chancery and the order to the customs officers to use the
new Book. It included also the revised duties on cloth
exported, and these were later given in the printed versions
of the Book.[1] Apart from this, the new Book was similar in
form to the Book of 1545. It listed the imports and exports
with their values, but now grouped them both in a rough
alphabetical order. Though the Book resembled its pre-
decessors, it was in fact a completely revised version. It
listed some 1100 commodities, or about 300 more than were
in the Book of 1545. The new items were mostly imports.
They included many drugs, several varieties of foreign cloth,
haberdashery wares, and miscellaneous manufactured goods
ranging from andirons to warming pans. Both the old and
the new items reflected the wide diversity of English imports at this time. Indeed of the 1100 commodities, only 67
were classed as exports. This, too, reflected the concentration
of the export trade on a few staple commodities. It should be
remembered, however, that exports 'not mentioned among
the rates for the subsidies or poundage outwards' were to be
rated 'according unto the values and prices of the same goods
mentioned in this book among the rates for the subsidie and
poundage inwards'. It was in accordance with this provision
that re-exports were rated.

The revision of 1558 was more important for its new
valuations than for its inclusion of new items. At last the
proposals of 1536 and 1552 were put into effect by a wholesale revaluation of both imports and exports. It is possible to
compare the valuations of 1545 with those of 1558 for 570
commodities.[2] In 525 cases the valuations were raised in

[1] Infra, pp. 70–4.
[2] These do not include a number of commodities which do not seem to be
strictly comparable.

1558; the rises ranged from 12·5 per cent for 'Cullen silk' to 1100 per cent for 'cushen cloths'. In 33 cases the valuations remained unchanged. These included imported apples, unbound books, bowstaves, carving knives, coral, deals, lemons, quernstones, and whitings. In 12 cases the valuations were reduced in 1558. These included bosses for bridles, reduced from 12s. to 10s. the dozen; brickstones, reduced from 10s. to 6s. 8d. the thousand; hawks called falcons, reduced from 40s. to 26s. 8d. the hawk; isinglass, reduced from 4d. to 2d. lb.; matches for gunners, reduced from 4d. to 2d. lb.; quails, reduced from 20s. to 4s. dozen; and tenterhooks, reduced from 10s. to 2s. 6d. the thousand.

It is usually assumed that the Book of Rates of 1558 increased the valuations of goods by an average of about 75 per cent. Gras first gave currency to this figure in comparing the 'average valuation' of goods in the Books of 1558, 1582, and 1590 with the average in the Books of 1507 and 1545.[1] Dietz repeated this in a slightly different form. In comparing the valuations in the Book of 1558 with those in the earlier Books, he thought that 'a straight average would give at least 75 per cent increase'.[2] This estimate of 75 per cent was probably based on an impression rather than on an actual calculation, for Gras had not seen a complete version of the Book of 1558, and Dietz seems to have been copying Gras. The estimate seems in fact to be too low. The average increase in valuations on the 570 commodities was 118·8 per cent. Thus it is clear that the revision of 1558 brought a more substantial increase in valuations than has hitherto been thought. Unfortunately the new valuations themselves are not easy to interpret.

The valuations of 1558 present two problems: did they

[1] Gras, p. 125.
[2] F. C. Dietz, *English public finance, 1558–1641*, p. 307 n. 3.

represent genuine values at that time, and were they subsequently modified to take account of changing prices? Some light might be thrown on the first problem if it were known how the valuations of 1558 were arrived at. Unfortunately the only evidence on this point is the statement that the Crown had 'caused the pryses and values of all maner of goodes and marchaundyse lyable to the payment of the saide subsydie or pondage to be substantyally and partyculerly inquired and examyned aswell by the othes of credible personnes thereunto called and sworne as by other due and convenyent meanes'.[1] This is not very illuminating, though it does suggest that the valuations were based in part on statements made by merchants under oath. Merchants were interested parties, but it is difficult to see who else the 'credible personnes' could be. Even so, it is impossible to tell how the valuations were arrived at. It is necessary, therefore, to examine the valuations themselves in an attempt to see whether they represented what were later called real values.

The official view was clearly that goods remained undervalued even after the increases of 1558. In 1559 the French complained of the high duties which they said were levied on French goods. The Privy Council, in a letter of 13 June 1559, explained to Sir Nicholas Throgmorton that an additional poundage of 6d. in the £, levied as an imposition during the late war, had been removed. The French might claim that poundage had increased, but in fact it remained at 12d. in the £. It was true, however, 'that the rates of the prices of wares is sumewhat augmentyd (having at the first, the tyme so serving then, byn set at a very smale valu): and yet ar they not prysed skarce to half the price, that in very dede they be presently sold'. Throgmorton was to keep this

[1] Patent Rolls, 4 and 5 Philip and Mary, pt. 3, m. 12d.

information, 'touching this last valuation of wares', to himself, unless he should 'see good cause, or be pressed, by occasion of talke, to utter the same to sume good purpose'.[1] No doubt this alleged undervaluation might be a good bargaining counter in diplomacy, but was it true? Or was it just the usual official attempt to minimize increased taxation by claiming that the tax should really have been higher still? The answer to such questions must depend in part on what the Privy Council meant by 'half the price'. If it meant half the retail price, it was using an unjustifiable basis for its calculation; no one could really claim that ad valorem duties should be based on retail prices. If it meant half the whole-sale price, it would appear to have exaggerated the under-valuation.

Unless it is assumed that the valuations of 1558 were quite arbitrary or quite conventional, they must have been based on the wholesale prices prevailing at that time. No doubt the relationship between the valuations and wholesale prices would be a very rough and ready one. This is suggested by the number of goods that were valued at 3s. 4d. and its multiples. Such valuations expressed in terms of money of account are to be expected; they probably imply, not con-ventional values, but approximations to wholesale prices. The main difficulty is to determine the degree of approxima-tion; to determine, that is, whether the valuations roughly coincide with wholesale prices at a given point in time, or whether there was any systematic undervaluation or over-valuation. Superficially the solution appears simple: compare the valuations with wholesale prices and see whether they roughly coincide. In practice the solution is not simple, and that for two reasons. Firstly the prices of many goods are

[1] P. Forbes, *A full view of the public transactions in the reign of Q. Elizabeth*, i. 133.

not known; this is especially true of the large group of imported drugs. Secondly, where prices are available, they are usually retail rather than wholesale prices, and the margin between the two is not known. The choice lies, therefore, between abandoning any attempt to compare the valuations with wholesale prices, and trying to get some comparison based on such price material as is available. The latter seems worth attempting despite its risks and imperfections.

The valuations of 1558 covered about 1100 separate items. These included goods quoted in different sizes; for example, large looking glasses of crystal were valued at 40s. a dozen, small at 20s. a dozen. They may well have included a few exotic items that did not really exist. Of the 1100 items, it is possible to get prices for between 60 and 70. These prices do not all relate to the year 1558, but they come within the period of the late fifties and of the sixties.[1] They almost all appear to be retail prices. In two or three cases the prices are lower than the valuations. Thus among the exports, candles were valued at 4s. a dozen lb., whereas their price seems to have varied from 2s. to 3s. 6d. a dozen lb. Similarly, exported lead seems to have been somewhat overvalued. This was exceptional; in general the retail prices are higher than the valuations, as indeed they ought to be. Sometimes the difference is very great, especially among certain of the imports. Thus brimstone was valued at 6s. 8d. cwt., compared with a price of 28s. cwt.; carraway seeds were valued at 20s. cwt., but their retail price was apparently 1s. 4d. to 1s. 8d. lb.; train oil, valued at £5 a ton, cost the Navy £12 15s. a ton in 1566. Such disparities clearly represent undervaluations, not the difference between wholesale and retail prices. Again,

[1] Prices have been obtained from J. E. T. Rogers, *A history of agriculture and prices in England*, iii, iv, and Sir William Beveridge, *Prices and wages in England*, i.

they are exceptional. In general the valuations are lower than the prices, but not so much lower as to suggest that the valuations had no real relationship to wholesale prices. If any conclusion can be drawn from such an inadequate sample of prices, it is that the valuations of 1558 were very roughly based on wholesale prices. Moreover the evidence suggests, but it is inadequate to prove, that the valuations were on the whole rather lower than the wholesale prices. In other words, the valuations of 1558, with few exceptions, would make the duty of 12d. in the £ equal to a maximum of 5 per cent of the real value of exports and imports. It is probable that undervaluation brought the duty rather below 5 per cent.

The problem of relating the valuations of 1558 to current prices is clearly a difficult one, and one which cannot be completely solved. The second and allied problem, namely, were the valuations later modified to take account of changing prices, is much simpler. Here it is necessary to compare the valuations of 1558 with those in force later in Elizabeth's reign, and the existence of printed Books of Rates makes such a comparison possible.

The earliest printed Book of Rates for Elizabeth's reign, or at least the earliest that has survived, was issued in 1562.[1] This edition was not known to Gras, and indeed seems to have escaped attention altogether. It is apparently represented by a unique copy which originally belonged to William Cecil. Besides bearing Cecil's signature on the title-page, the Book contains a few notes or jottings by him.

---

[1] *The Rates of the Customhouse, Subsidye or Poundage, as wel for all kinde of Marchandise inwarde, as also Wolle, Clothes, and all other Merchaundise, outwarde in any of the Queens majesties Portes, Havens or Creekes, Stablished by an Act of Parliament in the first year of the rayne of Queene Mary newly corrected, amended and in many places enlarged.* London, 1562. The only copy of this edition is at Hatfield House, where it is classified among the Salisbury MSS. (*H.M.C. Salisbury*, xiii. 60).

Unfortunately Cecil's comments throw no light either on his own thought or on the contents of the book. The Book of Rates of 1562 repeats the valuations of 1558, as might indeed be expected. In about a dozen cases the valuations of 1562 differ from those of 1558, but in none of these cases does the difference seem to represent a genuine revaluation. Most of the differences are due to simple errors in printing. Thus 'crippin partlets with silk' were valued at 4*s.* a dozen in 1562, but this was merely an error for the £4 a dozen of 1558. Similarly 'wrests for virginals' were valued at 12*d.* a gross in 1562, but this was an error for the 12*s.* a gross of 1558. In subsequent Books of Rates these errors were corrected, though usually others were made in their place. One or two of the differences in valuations were not due to errors made in 1562, but to the correction of errors made in 1558. The best example of this is 'gum ceraphana', which was valued at £16 a lb. in 1558. This was plainly a mistake, and it was corrected to 16*d.* a lb. in 1562. Thus the four years from 1558 to 1562 saw no change in the valuations for customs purposes, and indeed no change was to be expected in so short a time, whatever had happened to prices in the interval. The interval had seen the re-coinage of 1560–1, but that does not appear to have had a deflationary effect which might temporarily have counteracted the general inflationary tendency of the period.

If the Book of Rates of 1562 appeared too soon after 1558 to have any bearing on the question of revaluations, that is not true of the Book which appeared twenty years later. Indeed in the interval a commission had been appointed to revise the Book of Rates. On 11 June 1577 this task had been given by letters patent to Sir Nicholas Bacon, Burghley, Sussex, Leicester, Sir Francis Walsingham, and Sir Walter Mildmay. These commissioners were to revise the list of

c

goods and the values assigned to such goods in 1558. They were to make a new list of goods and values, which was to be signed by the Queen and sent under the Great Seal to the Exchequer. Copies of this new list were to be sent to all the customs officers. It was specifically stated in the letters patent that the values of 1558 were still in force in 1577.[1] There does not seem to be any evidence that the commissioners of 1577 did in fact produce a revised Book of Rates. It might be argued that they took five years over the revision, and that the Book of 1582 was the result of their labours. This was not so however, for the Book of 1582 did not contain a revision of the rates of 1558. It seems inconceivable that the commissioners should have considered that no revision of any of the rates was necessary. Either the commissioners did not proceed with their task or they produced a revised Book which was not adopted.

The Book of Rates of 1582[2] was an improved and expanded version of that of 1562. It was improved by printing the imports and exports in a much more strictly alphabetical order. It was expanded by including information on weights and measures and by giving a long list of the duties known as scavage. The real interest and importance of the Book lie, however, in its valuations of goods imported and exported. These valuations or ratings were the same as those of 1558 and 1562. It is true that in about a dozen cases the valuations of 1582 differed from the earlier ones, but these differences

[1] Patent Rolls, 19 Eliz. I, pt. 12, m. 7d. I am indebted to Dr. N. J. Williams for this reference.

[2] Infra, pp. 1–86. Two copies of this Book exist: one in the Bodleian Library (Douce C 70), which is the one here reprinted; and one in Emmanuel College Library, Cambridge. This Book has often been assigned to 1583, and I myself have been guilty of so assigning it in the past. This error has arisen because the date on the title-page of the Bodleian copy is badly printed and could easily be read as 1583. The Bodleian experts, however, assure me that the date is 1582, and not 1583. The copy at Cambridge is also dated 1582.

were clearly mistakes of the printer. Thus tailors' shears were valued at 8*d*. a dozen instead of the 8*s*. a dozen of 1558 and 1562; this was again correctly given as 8*s*. in 1590. Similarly aniseed at 16*s*. 8*d*. cwt. was obviously a mistake for the 26*s*. 8*d*. cwt. of 1558, 1562, and 1590.

In one respect the list of imports and exports of 1582 did genuinely differ from the lists of 1558 and 1562. It was rather longer, for in the interval some new items had been added. There had been provision in the earlier Books of Rates for such additions to be valued 'upon the othe of the merchant in the presence of the Customer and Controuler for the time beeing until furder order shalbe taken therein by us and our Councel'. It is not clear whether the additions of 1582 were valued solely on the oath of the merchant or whether they were the result of further order taken by the Queen and the Privy Council. There does not seem to be any evidence that order had been taken by the Queen and the Privy Council. Indeed it seems likely that additions were made on the oath of the merchant and that no 'furder order' was taken until the Book of Rates as a whole was revised.

This machinery by which additional items could be valued was meant to cover both goods which had been accidentally omitted from the Book of Rates and goods which had only been imported or exported after the Book had been compiled. The additions made in 1582 seem to include both categories. Thus it seems likely that Spanish wool, iron pots, and tenon saws, which were first included among the imports in 1582, had in fact been imported before 1558 and had been accidentally omitted from the valuations of that year. The same may well be true of the masts, great and small, the Rhenish glasses, and the heath for brushes, which were also added in 1582. Other new items, however, appear to be goods which had only recently begun to form part of England's foreign trade. These included cochineal, a product of the New World,[1] and panele, a type of unrefined sugar imported from Morocco. The list of 1582 had thus been brought up to date by the addition of new items, but it had certainly not been brought up to date by the revaluation of goods which had figured in the lists of 1558 and 1562. No one could claim that such revaluation was unnecessary because prices had not changed in the interval; between 1558 and 1582 prices in general had risen considerably. Thus the Book of Rates of 1582 shows that no attempt had been made to adjust the valuations of 1558 to changing prices.

According to Sir Geoffrey Gilbert, a new edition of the Book of Rates was issued in 1586,[2] and certainly the *Oxford English Dictionary* quotes such an edition,[3] without, however, including it in the *Dictionary's* Bibliography.[4] No copy of this edition appears to be extant. It would seem that the *O.E.D.*'s quotations were really taken from the edition of 1582. A new edition was, however, brought out in 1590.[5] This was almost identical with the edition of 1582. The main differences were some new errors in printing and some corrections of earlier errors. There was no revision of valuations, though prices had continued to rise in the interval. Thus in

[1] The introduction of cochineal is discussed in R. L. Lee, 'American cochineal in European commerce, 1526–1625', *Journal of Modern History*, xxiii. 205–24.

[2] Sir Geoffrey Gilbert, *A treatise on the Court of Exchequer*, p. 224.

[3] See, for example, the quotations in *O.E.D.* under Tartar, Turmeric, etc.

[4] The Bibliography gives the editions of 1545 and 1582 (which is given as 1583).

[5] *The Rates of the Custome house. Reduced into a much better order for the redier finding of any thing therin contained, then at any time heertofore hath beene: and now againe newly corrected, enlarged and amended. Wherunto is also added the true difference and contents of waights and measures, with other things never before Imprinted.* London, 1590 (Brit. Mus. C 40 b. 29). This is the first of the Books to be paginated, but only the right-hand pages are numbered.

1590 most ad valorem duties were still levied on goods in accordance with valuations made more than thirty years before.

The growing discrepancy between current prices and the valuations of 1558 had been obvious long before 1590, but the proposed revision of 1577 had come to nothing, and it was apparently only in the last decade of the century that any further attempt to revise the Book of Rates was made. The only serious attempt seems to have been made in 1594. In a letter of 7 July 1599, Thomas Fanshaw, Queen's Remembrancer of the Exchequer, described to Sir Robert Cecil what had happened then. Four or five years ago, according to Fanshaw, the Queen had been informed that 'sundry kinds of merchandises' were undervalued, to her great loss, and some were overvalued. The Queen had therefore appointed Henry Billingsley, Richard Carmarden, and others of the Custom House, together with some merchants and Fanshaw himself, 'to peruse the old rates and to consider what new rates were fit to be set'. This body had met several times and had agreed upon various alterations and new rates, and had set them down in a book which Fanshaw and others had signed. It was, however, 'thought at that time inconvenient for her Majesty to ratify the same', for reasons which Fanshaw did 'not now remember'. He had heard nothing further of the matter until recently when one of the new Surveyors of the customs had asked him about it. Thus, as Fanshaw had pointed out earlier in his letter, the rates established by Mary in 1558 had 'ever since been answered, for anything I know to the contrary'.[1]

The revised 'book' of 1594 does not seem to have survived, and it would in any case have had no authority without ratification, but some of the proposed changes in valuations

[1] *H.M.C. Salisbury*, ix. 226.

were contained in an account or memorandum presented to
Burghley by Billingsley and Carmarden on 12 November
1594.[1] This listed the proposed changes in valuations under
three headings. The first contained 51[2] items which had been
included in the Book of Rates of 1558 and which were now
undervalued. Against each item was set the 'old rate' (i.e.
before the revision of 1558), the 'rate in force', the 'rate that
may be', and the increase in the yield from duties if the 'rate
that may be' were adopted. The increased yield was based on
the quantities of the goods imported into London between
Michaelmas 1593 and Michaelmas 1594. The most important
items on this list, from the point of view of the increased
revenue to be derived from increased valuations, were Seville
oil, great raisins, madder, green woad, soap ashes, flax,
pitch and tar, battery wares, thrown silk, and various sorts
of cloth. The cloth included most of the chief imported
varieties: fustians, Normandy canvas, lawns, cambrics, Hol-
lands, Munsters, and Osnabrücks. The proposed increases in
valuations varied greatly. Thus almonds should be raised
from 40s. to 50s. cwt., and raisins of the sun from 16s. 8d. to
18s. cwt. These were moderate increases compared with the
suggested raising of soap ashes from £3 to £6 the last and of
Spanish iron from £4 to £8 the ton. Even these were not the
greatest increases proposed: Seville oil should be raised from
£8 to £20 the ton and wainscot from £4 to £12 the hundred.
On rhubarb there was agreement that it was undervalued at
13s. 4d. lb., but some doubt as to its real value, which was
variously given as £2 and £5 lb. The average increase in
valuation over the whole 51 items was about 80 per cent. On
the basis of the London imports of 1593–4, the new valua-

[1] S.P.D. Eliz., ccl, nos. 30–2, contains three versions of this account;
the versions do not always agree. There is another version in Exch. K.R.
Customs Accounts, 196/7.
[2] Two of the items were merely different quantities of figs.

tions would bring in an additional revenue of £6171 5s. 3d. from the duty of 1s. in the £.

The second group of commodities in the documents of 1594 contained 18 items which were not in the Book of Rates of 1558 and which had been rated on the oaths of the merchants. These, too, were undervalued, and the list gave the proposed increases in values. These goods included indigo, cochineal, Meighborough deals, India hides, smalt, thread, and certain sorts of linen and cotton cloth. Again the proposed increases in valuations varied considerably. Indigo at 1s. 8d. lb. should be raised 20 per cent to 2s. lb.; Meighborough deals should also be raised 20 per cent from £3 6s. 8d. to £4 the hundred. At the other extreme, mockadoes at £1 the piece should be increased by 100 per cent to £2, and Cyprus thread from 5s. to 10s. lb. The average increase proposed was about 48 per cent. This would bring in an additional revenue of £1093 13s. 1d. on the basis of the London imports of 1593–4.

Finally there was a list of goods that were overvalued. The three versions of this list in the documents of 1594 show some differences, but apparently 18 items in all were thought to be overvalued. It was of course natural that, even during an inflationary period, certain goods should be overvalued, either because they had been overvalued initially or because their values had fallen in the interval. It was perhaps not very important that ambergris was said to be worth only 50s. oz., whereas it was rated at 60s., or that manna was worth only one-third of its valuation of 20s. lb. Such exotic products can hardly have been in great demand. The same was true of Venice gold and silver,[1] which was a gold or silver thread valued at 53s. 4d. lb., and worth only 40s., and

---

[1] *H.M.C. Salisbury*, viii. 545, gives the London imports from Christmas 1594 to Midsummer 1598.

Levant taffeta valued at 20*d*. a yard and worth only 14*d*. Other overvalued goods were of greater economic importance. They included such raw materials as alum, valued at 33*s*. 4*d*. cwt. and worth 22*s*. 8*d*., rough hemp, valued at 20*s*. cwt. and worth 13*s*. 4*d*., and Norway deals, valued at £10 the long hundred and worth £6. They included, too, some sugar and spice. The unrefined sugar called panele, which had first appeared in the 1582 Book of Rates, was valued at 33*s*. 4*d*. cwt. and was said to be worth only 26*s*. 8*d*. cwt. Muscovado and other coarse sugars, which were valued at £3 6*s*. 8*d*., the same rate as refined sugar, were said to be worth only 30*s*. cwt. It is probable that these unrefined sugars had been overvalued in the first place and had also been reduced in price through greater imports. The same may have been true of ginger, valued at £7 10*s*. cwt. and said to be worth only £3, and fusses of cloves, valued at 4*s*. lb. and worth 14*d*. Apart from cloves, the most overvalued items in the list were ginger dust at 7*d*. lb. and worth only 2*d*., and cassia fistula at £10 cwt. and worth only £2 10*s*. If it is not surprising that some goods were thought to be overvalued in 1594, it is certainly surprising that more goods were not thought to be undervalued. It would be rash, however, to assume that the lists submitted by Billingsley and Carmarden contained all the changes that it was proposed to make in the Book of Rates at that time.

Whatever changes it was proposed to make in 1594, it is clear that they were not made. Two years later Carmarden told Burghley that the Queen still had 'an intention hereafter to make an alteration of some rates in respect they are too low, wherein also some are too high, which are likewise to be brought lower'. Of the rates that needed to be brought down, that of alum was 'one of the chiefest'.[1] Nothing was

[1] *H.M.C.Salisbury*, vi. 174.

done. In a statement of 1602 it was still being pointed out that a new Book of Rates was necessary; although the value of goods had increased since Queen Mary's time, 'the customs had never increased, but had been collected by a Book of Rates made in Queen Mary's days'. As a result, Elizabeth had lost more than half a million pounds in revenue from customs. She should call in 'the old and false Book of Rates' and issue a new one.[1] She did not do so, for a revised Book of Rates was only issued by her successor in 1604.

The new Book of Rates of 1604[2] began by declaring that the valuations made in 1558 had remained in force throughout Elizabeth's reign; as a result, divers goods were now undervalued to the King's 'great losse', and divers were valued too highly, to the prejudice of the merchants. Moreover some goods had not been valued in the Book of 1558, but had been valued only by 'the oathes of them to whom the said goods, wares and marchandizes did belong'. Therefore a commission under the Great Seal had caused inquiry and examination to be made of 'reasonable and indifferent values and prices'. These 'reasonable and indifferent values and prices' had now been fixed, and they were to be used as the basis for the assessment of duties. The Book of Rates, which embodied this revision, contained many new items among both the imports and the exports. The imports now included such interesting things as ginger bread or 'pepper cakes' at 20s. a barrel and, much more important, 'tabacco leafe' at 6s. 8d. the pound. The exports included some goods which were really re-exports, such as train oil, but they also

[1] Ibid., xii. 565-6.
[2] *The Rates of Marchandizes as they are set downe in the Booke of Rates for the Custome and Subsidie of Poundage, and for the Custome of Clothes, the same being signed by the Kings Majestie, and sealed with the great Seale of England, and remaining in his Highnesse Court of Exchequer at Westminster, And by speciall commaundement from his Majestie published in Print, for the direction of such as it may concern.* London, 1604.

included many new types of English cloth, which were the products of the new drapery. Both the old and the new items were now more grouped together under such general headings as Drugs (over 200 of them), Fish, Furs, Fustians, and so on.

It is not possible to compare all the valuations of 1604 with those of Elizabeth's reign, for some of the items were quite new and others appear to have differed in type or quantity. Of the items that seem strictly comparable, 871 in all, the valuations of 590 remained unchanged in 1604, the valuations of 216 were increased, and the valuations of 65 were decreased. The valuations of the 216 were increased an average of 64 per cent. These increases included some, but not all, of those recommended in 1594. Thus soap ashes were raised from £3 to £6 the last and great raisins from 5s. to 13s. 4d. cwt., as had been recommended in 1594. On the other hand, Seville oil was raised from £8 to £16 a ton, not to £20 as recommended. In two or three cases, wrought flax and Holland cloth for example, the increase was greater than that recommended in 1594. The decrease in the valuations of the 65 items averaged 35 per cent. Here again the recommendations of 1594 were not always followed, though there is perhaps no very valid reason why they should have been. Rough hemp was reduced from 20s. to 13s. 4d. cwt. as recommended in 1594, but alum was reduced from 33s. 4d. to 20s. cwt., not 22s. 8d. as recommended. No change was made in the valuation of panele, ambergris, and Venice gold and silver, though all were said to be overvalued in 1594.

It must be admitted that the revision of 1604 is not very easy to understand. It is easy enough to see why new items should have been added and why some old and perhaps mythical commodities should have disappeared from the list, but it is difficult to see why so many valuations remained unchanged. Over the whole 871 items where comparison with earlier valuations is possible, the average increase in the valuations was only 13·17 per cent. This is in marked contrast to the 118 per cent increase made in 1558. Prices may have risen more between 1507 and 1558 than between 1558 and 1604, but no one could seriously claim that the revised valuations of 1604 took adequate account of the rise in prices during Elizabeth's reign. The increased use of impositions by James I, as a method of expanding his customs revenue, was perhaps a recognition of this.

4. The Level of Duties

A study of the Books of Rates shows that the valuations of 1558 were not increased until 1604. Thus throughout Elizabeth's reign the ad valorem duty of 1s. in the £ was levied on goods to which, in practice, a fixed value had been assigned in 1558. This fixed value took no account of the changing price of goods, and there is no doubt that prices rose substantially between 1558 and 1604. The valuations of 1558 had in fact fossilized into official values which, with rising prices, lagged behind real values. When, at a time of rising prices, fixed ad valorem duties are levied on goods to which a fixed value has been assigned, those duties in practice become lighter and lighter; they come to represent, that is, a smaller percentage of the real value of the goods. Indeed this must happen unless the goods have been initially overvalued, and there seems no evidence that this had been done in 1558. There is evidence, however, that goods had become undervalued after that date. This evidence rests partly on the general trend of prices, which need not be elaborated here, and partly on specific examples covering certain exports and imports during the period.

Specific examples of undervaluation can be obtained by comparing the valuation of cargoes, or parts of cargoes, for customs purposes with the real values of the goods concerned. This is a laborious process, seriously hampered by the scarcity of good price material, but it can be applied on a limited scale. Thus part of a cargo imported from Russia in 1587 was worth about £12,156 according to the valuations of the Book of Rates, but its real value may have been about £23,232.[1] Even if the latter figure is too high, being based partly on retail prices, there is no doubt that these imports were seriously undervalued for customs purposes. Similarly part of a cargo imported from the Levant in 1588 was officially valued at £15,390, but its real value was about £40,038.[2] In this case the duty of 1s. in the £ was equivalent, not to 5 per cent, but to 1·6 per cent ad valorem. This type of comparison of official with real values was sometimes made by contemporaries, though they did not use these terms in describing the values. Thus a list of imports for 1570, which contains 38 items, gives their value as £45,356 18s., and their value as rated by the customs as £27,304 13s. Omitting wine, valued at £2890, from the list, the 1s. in the £ duty on the remaining items would represent about 3 per cent ad valorem.[3] Too much reliance should not perhaps be placed on this list of imports, which was part of the usual attempt to prove an unfavourable balance of trade, but the list does suggest that even by 1570 the revised valuations of 1558 had failed to keep pace with prices.

Finally it is instructive to examine a more concrete case, where the actual price paid by or obtained by the merchant

[1] T. S. Willan, *The early history of the Russia Company*, p. 182.
[2] T. S. Willan, 'Some aspects of English trade with the Levant in the sixteenth century', *English Historical Review*, lxx. 408.
[3] Cotton MSS., Titus B IV, f. 225; H. Hall, *A history of the custom-revenue in England*, ii. 243–4.

for goods can be compared with the actual duties paid on those goods. The partnership which traded with Morocco between 1585 and 1589 has left detailed accounts of its transactions,[1] and from these accounts such a comparison can be made. The partnership's export of short cloths has already been mentioned,[2] but such cloth formed only a small part of its trade. In 1585, in addition to short cloths, the partners exported iron, lead, tin, wire, pewter, saffron, and various types of continental cloth. The iron amounted to 143 tons 16 cwt. 91 lb., bought at prices ranging from £10 10s. to £12 6s. 8d. the ton, and totalling £1582 15s. 6d. Duty was paid on only 132 tons, officially valued at £8 a ton; the duty of 1s. in the £ comes to £52 16s., or 3·32 per cent ad valorem. This payment of duty on rather less than the amount of goods actually exported was a common feature of the partners' shipments. It would be interesting to know whether the practice was general, for it had, of course, the effect of reducing the duties in ad valorem terms. Thus the partners shipped 67 fodder 34 lb. of lead, bought at from £9 to £9 6s. 8d. the fodder, and totalling £624 1s. 1d. They paid duty on 61 fodder, officially valued at £8 a fodder; the duty works out at 3·91 per cent ad valorem. On tin, bought at £2 18s. to £3 4s. cwt., compared with an official value of 33s. 4d. cwt. for Cornish and 30s. cwt. for Devonshire tin, they paid duty on 192 cwt. out of a total shipment of 214 cwt. 7 lb. Here the duty paid was only 2·74 per cent ad valorem. On wire, some 10 cwt. of various sorts, the duty was 2·9 per cent. ad valorem, and on pewter it was 2·5 per cent. The saffron amounted to 170 lb., bought at 18s. lb. (official value 13s. 4d. lb.); duty was paid on 150 lb. and equalled 3·26 per cent ad valorem.

[1] Evelyn MSS., 155 (Christ Church Library, Oxford); cf. supra, pp. xvi–xvii.
[2] Supra, pp. xvi–xvii.

The re-exported continental cloth had, of course, the same official value when exported as it had had when originally imported. That value seems to have been well below the wholesale price of the cloth. Thus 10,600 ells of white Normandy canvas, which were officially valued at £353 6s. 8d., actually cost the partners £1483 10s. They paid £17 13s. 4d. in duty, or 1·19 per cent ad valorem. The 3163½ ells of broad Hamburg cloth, which cost £171 5s. 7d., were officially valued at £100; the duty paid was £5 or 2·92 per cent ad valorem. Finally 98 half pieces of Holland cloth, which cost £241 14s. 6d., were officially valued at £60; the duty was £3 or 1·24 per cent ad valorem.

The goods imported from Morocco by the partners consisted largely of sugar, almonds, indigo, and saltpetre. Sugar in various forms was the most important of these. In 1585 the partners imported 217½ cwt. of sugar which cost at the first hand £787 6s. 10d. They paid duty on 204 cwt., which were officially valued at £3 6s. 8d. cwt. In this case the duty amounted to 4·3 per cent of the prime cost and 3·3 per cent of the amount actually obtained for the sugar when it was sold in London. Seven tons of unrefined sugar called ramels were also imported. They were sold for £9 a ton, which was less than they cost and less than their official value of £10 a ton. The duty came to 5·5 per cent of the selling price. During their second year's trading, from 1586 to 1587, the partners imported 103 cwt. almonds, though they seem only to have paid duty on 74 cwt. Not only was there this discrepancy between the amount imported and the amount upon which duty was paid, but also the 74 cwt. were valued at £1 6s. 8d. cwt. by the customs officers instead of at the 40s. of the Book of Rates. It is hardly surprising that the duty paid was equal to only 2·7 per cent of the cost of the almonds in Morocco.

Even so, they were sold at a loss in London, which made the duty equal to 2·9 per cent of the selling price. Indigo and saltpetre were imported in 1587–8, but in their cases it is difficult to determine the duties in ad valorem terms. Indigo was apparently valued officially at £10 cwt.; it cost £10 8s. cwt. in Morocco and was sold for only £6 13s. 4d. cwt in London. Thus the duty was 4·8 per cent of the buying price and 7·5 per cent of the selling price. These figures lend little support to the claim made in 1594 that indigo was among the undervalued imports. Finally saltpetre, which cost 48s. to 60s. cwt. in Morocco, was officially valued at 30s. cwt., making the duty 3·1 to 2·5 per cent of the buying price. It was sold for £3 6s. 8d. to £3 10s. cwt. in London, making the duty just over 2 per cent of the selling price.

This evidence derived from the Moroccan trade supports the view that the duties actually paid by Elizabethan merchants were very low ones. Indeed over the whole range of English foreign trade it was only certain of the specific duties that were high. No one would deny that the duties on wool and wine were high; the same was perhaps true of leather in so far as it was allowed to be exported at all. The main specific duty on exports, that on cloth, was not high, at least for native merchants. Similarly the ad valorem duties, which covered most imports and some exports, were nominally only 5 per cent of the value of the goods. This was not a high duty even when it was calculated on the real value of the goods. In practice, as prices rose and official values remained unchanged, the ad valorem duties seem usually to have fallen below 5 per cent, and often well below. To a modern protectionist, on either side of the Atlantic, such duties would not be regarded as protective. Indeed if he forgot the wine and the wool, a modern protectionist might well regard Elizabethan England as almost a free trade country.

5. CONCLUSION

An examination of the Books of Rates as the basis for the assessment of customs duties leads to the conclusion that Elizabethan England was on the whole a country of low duties. This conclusion should lead in turn to some reconsideration of the question of smuggling and to some re-examination of certain aspects of economic policy.

On the question of smuggling little need be said here, except to repeat the obvious fact that smuggling is usually a response either to prohibitions or to high duties. Some prohibitions and some high duties existed during Elizabeth's reign, and the smuggling of corn outwards and of wine inwards no doubt reflected their existence. For most goods, however, the duties were so low that they seem hardly worth evading. It must have needed a nice calculation to balance the cost of paying ad valorem duties of less than 5 per cent with the cost of evading such duties, for evasion itself involved some cost in bribery and corruption and perhaps also some increased transport charges when goods were shipped from obscure creeks. No doubt for some goods in some places at certain times the balance tipped in favour of smuggling; indeed the whole system of duties here examined suggests that such smuggling would be highly selective. There is nothing novel in such a conclusion, for smuggling has always been selective, but it does lead to one further consideration. If smuggling was selective, then some statistics of Elizabethan foreign trade may be more accurate than others. No doubt it is difficult to separate the statistical sheep from the statistical goats, but it may be better to attempt that than to condemn them all to the slaughter.

The relationship of low duties to the general economic policy of the period raises complex issues. Some have regarded that general economic policy as mercantilist, and it is usually assumed that mercantilism included the protection of native industries. Protection of industry can take many forms, but again it is usually assumed that protection in the tariff sense is an essential part of what Heckscher describes as 'Mercantilism as a system of protection'. Here it is not necessary to revive the controversy over the existence and meaning of mercantilism, but if Elizabeth's economic policy is described as mercantilist, it is clear that tariff protection played little part in that mercantilism. In general Elizabethan customs duties were too low to afford any real protection to English industry. Nor were the few high duties protective in the ordinary sense. There was no native wine industry to protect. There was a native cloth industry, but its protection consisted in safeguarding its chief raw material, wool, by a heavy export duty and not in imposing heavy import duties on competing continental cloth.

It might be claimed that, despite low import duties, native industry was protected in other ways. There is some truth in this view, but it is very easy to exaggerate the amount of protection. Thus the prohibition on the export of bell metal, copper, and leather[1] could be represented as a measure for safeguarding the supply of these raw materials for native industry. It may have been that, but the grant of licences for the export of these commodities suggests a less high-minded motive. Similarly there was some prohibition on imports, but it did not amount to much. The patents of monopoly which gave the patentee the sole right to manufacture a particular article, very rarely gave him the right to prohibit imports of that article. Nor did they protect his 'infant industry' by raising the import duties on foreign and competing goods. It was possible, of course, to prohibit

---

[1] 2/3 Ed. VI, c. 37; 1 Eliz., c. 10.

D

import by statute, but this was very rarely done. Indeed there seems to be only one clear case where an industry was given protection by a statutory prohibition of import. In 1597 the makers of woolcards were protected by an Act which prohibited the import of woolcards, though it did not prohibit the import of the wire from which they were made.[1] This Act seems to have been the response to a particular pressure group rather than an expression of a general protective policy.

Finally, what of that 'mercantilist' measure of 1563, the 'Acte for the avoyding of dyvers forreyne wares made by handye craftesmen beyonde the seas', which prohibited the import of a range of manufactured goods, including girdles, rapiers, knives, hilts, scabbards, bits, and pins?[2] The purpose of this Act, as stated in the preamble, was the protection of native industry, especially urban industry. The Act may have had that purpose, it is usually assumed that it had, but that is by no means certain. The Act may have been one of the early moves in the dispute with the Low Countries, which culminated in the commercial crisis of 1563–4; it was from the Low Countries that the articles enumerated in the Act usually came. The ending of the commercial crisis in 1564 seems to have made the Act a dead letter, despite its subsequent history. The Act, as passed in 1563, was to be in force until the end of the next Parliament. It was renewed in 1571 with the proviso that it was not to be prejudicial to any treaty of intercourse then in force between the Queen and other rulers.[3] This proviso was repealed in 1572[4] and it does not appear in the Act as subsequently renewed.[5]

---

[1] 39 Eliz., c. 14.
[2] 5 Eliz., c. 7; R. H. Tawney and E. Power, *Tudor economic documents*, i. 126–7.   [3] 13 Eliz., c. 25.   [4] 14 Eliz., c. 11.
[5] 27 Eliz., c. 11; 29 Eliz., c. 5; 31 Eliz., c. 10; 35 Eliz., c. 7; 39 Eliz., c. 18; 43 Eliz., c. 9.

Despite the repeal of this proviso, it is clear that the Act was interpreted as if the proviso were still in force, at least as regards trade with the Low Countries. Thus in 1591, when an informer, John Leake, brought an action against two merchant strangers for importing pins from the Low Countries contrary to the Act, the Privy Council instructed the Chief Baron and the Barons of the Exchequer to dismiss the suit. The Privy Council explained that when the Act was made and executed there was an ordinance forbidding the import of cloth into the Low Countries, which led to an interruption of commercial intercourse. In the negotiations which brought that interruption to an end, the Commissioners had agreed that the Act should not apply to subjects of the Low Countries.[1] This view that the Act did not apply to the Low Countries, and had not so applied since 1564, had in fact been affirmed by the Privy Council five years before Leake did his informing.[2] Thus the Act did not apply to the chief area from which the prohibited goods came, and certainly the Port Books show such goods, especially pins, coming in without restraint.[3] It is not surprising that the pinmakers and needlemakers of London petitioned in 1597 for the Act to be enforced, alleging that £40,000 worth of pins and needles were imported every year.[4] It is not necessary to accept this figure, one of those good round numbers beloved of contemporary petitioners, but it is necessary to realize that the Act of 1563 can have done little to protect English industry. No decayed towns can have risen from their ruins as a result of it.

A study of the Elizabethan tariff system suggests that most duties were too low to be protective and that supplementary measures such as the prohibition of imports or the licensing

---

[1] *A.P.C. 1591*, pp. 176–7.   [2] Ibid., *1586–7*, pp. 189–90.
[3] E.g. Exch. K.R. Port Books, 8/1.   [4] *H.M.C. Salisbury*, vii. 545.

of exports can have done little to foster industrial growth. Whatever stimulated the growth of those large-scale industries, which Professor Nef has described and whose importance has been so much exaggerated, it can hardly have been the shelter of tariff walls. Yet contemporaries realized the possibility of fostering industry through protection. The Doctor in *A discourse of the common weal* advanced an 'infant industry' argument for encouraging the manufacture of paper in England; the import of foreign paper was to be either prohibited or hindered by such high duties that 'oure men might afford theire paper better cheape then straungers might doe theires, the custome considered'.[1] The result of this plea was neither prohibition nor protection, but the continued import of paper and, much later, the grant of a patent to John Spilman for its manufacture.[2]

The maintenance of low duties is somewhat surprising in view of the contemporary concern over foreign competition, the decay of urban industry, and the problem of employment. It is even more surprising in view of the contemporary concern over the balance of trade. The desire for a favourable balance of trade, with its excess of exports over imports and its resulting inflow of bullion, was almost obsessional at this time. It was a commonplace to maintain with William Cecil that 'nothyng robbeth the realm of England, but whan moore marchandisees is brought in to the realme than is carryed forth'.[3] It was necessary for anxious statesmen to demand elaborate statistics showing the state of the balance.[4] Even simpler souls with no statistical bent could join in these ritualistic exercises by drawing up detailed lists of 'necessary' and 'superfluous' imports. It may not be obvious

[1] *A discourse of the common weal*, ed. E. Lamond, p. 66.
[2] D. C. Coleman, *The British paper industry, 1495–1860*, pp. 43–8.
[3] R. H. Tawney and E. Power, *Tudor economic documents*, ii. 124.
[4] E.g. Lans. MSS., 81, no. 37.

now why sugar candy was considered 'necessary' and canvas was considered 'superfluous',[1] but clearly people thought they knew what need, and what need not, be imported. Perhaps they did, but their calculations and classifications led to very little attempt to exclude the superfluous. They did not use the tariff as a method of exclusion; they did not place high duties on luxuries, except in the case of wine. They did not in fact use the tariff as a means of manipulating the balance of trade and making it more favourable.

This failure to use the tariff as a manipulator of foreign trade can hardly be ascribed to administrative difficulties. Such a use would not have involved greater complexities than already existed in a customs system which combined specific and ad valorem duties, a distinction between alien and native merchants, and special impositions on selected commodities. Clearly the explanation must be sought elsewhere. It must be sought in the consequences that might have followed from raising duties so high as to exclude some of those luxury imports which, according to contemporaries, contributed to an unfavourable balance of trade.

High duties which prohibited or hindered the import of particular goods would almost certainly bring a decline in customs revenue. When the Doctor in *A discourse of the common weal* pleaded for goods to be made at home rather than imported, the Knight was quick to point out 'if such ware weare made with in the Realme, then the kinges custome should be lesse'. To this the Doctor could only reply that 'the kinges attorney' should regard 'the proffitt that should come after' from the 'inestimable treasure' that 'should be saved with in the Realme'.[2] The Crown, however, was not concerned with some vague future profit, but with the

[1] H. Hall, *A history of the custom-revenue in England*, ii. 236–42.
[2] *A discourse of the common weal*, ed. E. Lamond, p. 66.

concrete day-to-day problem of finding enough money to run the state. In that race with rising expenditure, the yield of customs duties ranked with the yield from crown lands as one of the two great pillars of the ordinary revenue. Any measure which reduced the revenue from customs duties would mean greater dependence on parliamentary taxation and so on Parliament itself. That was not an outcome that Elizabeth could regard with equanimity. In any conflict between fiscalism and some general economic measure which might stimulate native industry or secure a more favourable balance of trade, it was fiscalism that won.

Loss of customs revenue was not the only possible disadvantage from a system of protective duties. Such duties might lead to retaliation, as again the Knight was quick to point out. And again the Doctor could only reply, rather unconvincingly, that 'oure stuffe is necessarie to theim', whereas many imports 'might be better spared of us then retained of theim'.[1] It might be a comforting belief that foreigners could not do without our exports while we could do without theirs, but a government constantly worried about the 'vent', especially of cloth, might not be prepared to put the belief to a practical test. It might not be prepared to put high duties on imported luxuries in case that led to a decline in the export of cloth. That decline would obviously not promote a more favourable balance of trade and it would lead to unemployment and unrest in the cloth-making districts. It was about such unemployment and unrest that the Crown was particularly sensitive, as the depression of 1586–7 showed. If the import of luxuries helped the export of cloth, it was better to maintain low duties on luxuries than to exclude them in the hope of securing thereby a more favourable balance of trade. One man, he was pro-

[1] *A discourse of the common weal*, ed. E. Lamond, pp. 67–8.

bably Roger Bodenham, saw the matter in this light. Writing
in 1571 on ways to increase the wealth of the country, he
gave a list of the chief exports and then of the chief imports
by countries. 'Nowe it followeth to be considered', he
continued, 'what we doo spende of the comodities of everie
of the said countries, and what they doo spende of ours, and
which of the said countries is most needfull, and which
least, and howe to provide therein. It is also to be considered
that althoughe other countries doo make many trifles which
as some saie we have no neede of, yet are they not to be forbidden because, if they shall not be suffred to sell their trifles
they cannot buy our good wares. For as thutteraunce of
thone is the cause of the uttraunce of thother, so is it needfull
to all sortes to sell the one for to buy the other. Whereby
all realmes be set a woorke, the people live thereby, and
princies customes greatlie increased.' [1]

More than forty years ago, in introducing his collection of
documents on the customs system, Gras wrote that 'the
study of this subject of the book of rates and of customs
valuations in general is indispensable to a proper under-
standing of the customs documents'.[2] That is true, for only
from a study of the Books of Rates can the basic features of
the Elizabethan tariff system be appreciated. Such a study
shows that, with some few exceptions, the duties levied on
exports and imports were low. Their purpose was to raise
revenue and not to protect industry or to secure a more
favourable balance of trade. This fact may be of some importance when the Crown's economic policy comes to be
reconsidered; it will lend little support to the view that
Elizabethan England had a planned economy.

[1] Lans. MSS., 100, no. 25. The document is endorsed 'Mr Bodnam'.
[2] Gras, p. 129.

The Rates of

the Custome house reduced into a much
better order for the redier finding of
any thing therin contained: then
at any time heertofore hath
been, and now again cor
rected enlarged and amended.
Wherunto is also added the true diffe
rence and contents of waights and
measures, with other things
never before Imprinted.

Imprinted at
London at the long shop adjoyning un
to Saint Mildreds Church in the
Pultrie by John Allde,
1582.

To the Reader

Heer hast thou (gentle Reder) the Rates of the Custome house that is to say, the Subsidie or poundage for all maner of merchandise aswel outwards as inwards, in any of the Queenes majesties Ports, Havens or Creeks established by an act of Parlement made in the first yeer of Queene Mary, and at this time standeth in strength.

And where as many things in the former Impressions stood confusedly and so out of order, that a man often times should have much to doo to finde some things therin contained: so now maist you finde any thing heerin with small seeking, considering not only the first letter of every name but also the second letter in the same name. As for example Abces is the first wherin you shall finde A. before B. and the next after Abces is Acasia wherin is A before C. and so foorth after the order of the Alphabet shalt you finde it thorowout. Farwel.

Rates inwards for the Subsidie.

Abces[1] the groce containing xij dosen in paper	iij*s*.
Abces the M after the rate of the groce	
Abces in parchment the groce	vi*s*.
Abces in Parchment the M after the rate of the groce	
Acasia[2] the pound	xii*d*.
Acornes[3] the pound	xvi*d*.
Adces[4] for Coopers the dosen	vi*s*.
Agarick[5] the pound	iii*s*. iiij*d*.
Agaricum the pound	iij*s*. iiij*d*.
Aglets[6] or Buttons for Childrens caps, the dosen[7]	v*s*.
Aglets or Buttons for other Caps of Copper the groce	iij*s*. iiij*d*.
Agnus castus[8] the pound	iiij*d*.
Alasicatrina[9] the pound	iij*s*. iii*d*.
Alasicatrina the C containining[10] v.xx	xvi*l*. xiii*s*. iiij*d*.
Alfany[11] the pound	xii*d*.

---

[1] ABCs or spelling-books.

[2] Acacia: probably not gum acacia, but the inspissated juice of the unripe fruit of species of acacia and mimosa, used as a drug.

[3] The 1558 Book of Rates has acorus, which makes better sense. Acorus is a genus of plants, including the sweet flag or galingale.

[4] Adzes.　　　　　　　　　　[5] Agaric, a purgative.

[6] Metallic tags, pendents, or spangles.

[7] A mistake for gross, which is the quantity given in the 1558 and 1562 Books of Rates.

[8] A herb, once believed to be a preservative of chastity, and later used in the cure of venereal diseases (Pomet, p. 13).

[9] Aloe cicotrina or succotrina, from the island of Socotra in the Indian Ocean; used as a purgative.　　　　[10] *Sic*.

[11] The 1604 Book of Rates has alcanet, so presumably alfany was alkanet, a red dye obtained from the root of a plant of that name.

Algares[1] for Carpenters the groce of all sortes	x*s.*
Albanum[2] the pound	viij*d.*
Alome[3] the c. containing v.xx and xii li.	xxxiij*s.* iiij*d.*
Almain rivets[4] the harnes	vi*s.* viiij*d.*
Almonds the bale containing iii C weight	vi*l.*
Almonds the bale containing v.xx xii li.	xl*s.*
Aloes the c. containing v.xx	x*l.*
Amber the mast containing ij li. di.	xxxiij*s.* iiij*d.*
Amber the pound	xiij*s.* iiij*d.*
Amber greece[5] the unce	iii*l.*
Amonium[6] the pound	ii*s.* vi*d.*
Anacardie[7] the pound	xvj*d.*
Andlets[8] called mailes the c. contayning v.xx li.	l*s.*
Andlets called mailes the li.	vi*d.*
Anniseeds[9] the c. containing v.xx xii li.	xvi*s.* viii*d.*[10]
Antimonium[11] the c li. containing v.xx	xvi*s.* viii*d.*[12]
Appuls the bushel	iiij*d.*
Appuls the barrel containing iij bushels	xii*d.*
Appuls called pippins or reinets[13] the barel iij Bushels	iii*s.*
Appuls called pippins or reinets the bushel	xij*d.*

---

[1] Augers.

[2] Ebenus, i.e. ebony; perhaps used as a drug, for according to Pomet (p. 71), the sap of ebony, infused in water, was thought to have a purgative quality, which would cure venereal disease.

[3] Alum, a mineral salt; its chief use was as a mordant in dyeing.

[4] Light armour, made flexible by overlapping plates sliding on rivets.

[5] Ambergris.

[6] Probably a spice from the aromatic amomum plant.

[7] Anacard, the nut of the cashew tree.

[8] Anlets, small rings, as those used in ring-mail.

[9] Aniseeds were used in medicine, confectionery, and perfumes.

[10] A mistake for xxvj*s.* viij*d.*, which is the figure given in the 1558, 1562, and 1590 Books of Rates.

[11] Antimony.

[12] A mistake for xvj*s.*, which is the figure given in the 1558, 1562, and 1590 Books of Rates.

[13] Rennets, dessert apples of French origin.

Aquavite[1] the barrel	xl*s.*
Argall[2] red the c. containing v.xx xij li.	xx*s.*
Argall white called winestone[3] the c. containing v.xx xij li.	xxiij*s.* iiij*d.*[4]
Argentum sublime[5] the pound	ij*s.*
Argentum sublime the c. containing v.xx	x*l.*
Armines[6] the timber containing xl skinnes	xx*s.*
Armoniacum[7] the pound	xij*d.*
Arras[8] the flemish elle	xl*s.*
Arrowes[9] for Truncks the groce	vi*s.* viij*d.*
Arsenick the C containing v.xx li.	xlj*s.* viij*d.*
Arsenick the pound	v*d.*
Aspatum[10] the pound	vi*d.*
Assafetida[11] the c containing v.xx xij li.	v*l.*
Assafetida the pound	xij*d.*
Ashes called Pot ashes[12] the Barrel containing ii C at v.xx the C	l*s.*
Ashes called pot Ashes the Last containing xii Barrels	xxx*l.*
Ashes called pot ashes the li.	iij*d.*

---

[1] Aqua-vitae.

[2] Argol, the crude bitartrate of potassium, which, when purified, becomes cream of tartar.

[3] The deposit of crude tartar or argol found in wine-casks.

[4] A mistake for xxiij*s.*, which is the figure given in the 1558, 1562, and 1590 Books of Rates.

[5] Probably mercury sublimate.

[6] Ermines.

[7] Ammoniacum or gum ammoniac, used in medicine.

[8] Tapestry, from Arras in Artois.

[9] Probably darts for shooting from a hollow tube or trunk (cf. infra, p. 62).

[10] Aspalathus, a genus of African shrubs, or the fragrant wood of some of its species.

[11] Asafoetida, a resinous gum used in cookery and medicine.

[12] A crude form of potassium carbonate made by 'lixiviating the ashes of terrestrial vegetables, and evaporating the solution in large iron pans or pots' (*O.E.D.*).

Ashes called wood or sope Ashes[1] the last
    containing xii Barrels   iii*l.*
Astrologia[2] Rotunda the C containing v.xx
    xii li.   xiij*s*. iiij*d*.
Aule[3] blades called blades for Aules the M   vi*s*. viii*d*.
Aule hafts called hafts for Aules the M   viii*s*.
Aundiorns[4] of Iron the pair   vi*s*. vij*d*.
Aundiorns of Latten[5] the pair   xxxiij*s*. iiij*d*.
Axes or Hatchets the dosen   iij*s*. iiii*d*.
Azarum[6] the pound   vi*d*.

B

Babyes or Puppets for Children the groce   vi*s*. viii*d*.
Badger skins the skin   xii*d*.
Bags with locks the dosen   xxiiij*s*.
Bags with steele Rings without locks, the
    dosen   xvi*s*.
Bayes[7] the C containing v.xx xij li.   xiij*s*. iiii*d*.
Balista[8] the pound   ij*s*.
Ballances called golde Ballances the groce   xl*s*.
Ballances called unce Ballances the groce   xx*s*.
Ballances the sorte containing iiii dosen   xxvi*s*. vij*d*.
Balles called Tennis balles the fat containing
    xxM   xx*l*.
Balles called Tennis balles the thousand   xx*s*.
Balles look washing Balles
Balme Glasses the groce   iij*s*. iiij*d*.

---

[1] Ashes from burnt wood which provided the alkaline base for soap.
[2] Astrologe, the herb aristolochia.
[3] Awl.   [4] Andirons.
[5] A mixed metal of yellow colour, either identical with or very like brass.
[6] Probably a medicament obtained from the asarum plant.
[7] Presumably bayberries, as in the 1604 Book of Rates.
[8] Balaustine, the flower of the wild pomegranate, used when dried as an astringent; the 1604 Book of Rates has balaustium.

Bands look Flaunders bands

Bankers of Verdure[1] the dosen peeces   xl*s.*

Barrels look emptie barrels

Basel[2] lether the dosen   viii*s.*

baserons[3] the c.   xxvi*s.* viii*d.*

bast[4] or strawe hats knotted the dosen   iii*s.* iiii*d.*

bast or strawe hats the dosen   viij*d.*

bast hats the M   xl*s.*

bast ropes the rope   vi*d.*

bast ropes the bundel   v*s.*

bast ropes the c. containing v.xx xii li.   viii*s.*

bast ropes the shock containing lx ropes   iii*l.*

Battery[5] or Kettles the c. containing v.xx xii li.   xl*s.*

Beades of bone the groce   xx*s.*

Beads of box the groce   xx*s.*

Beads of Christall the M   xl*s.*

Beades of wood of all sortes the groce   v*s.*

Beares living the bear   xx*s.*

Beares skinnes the skin black   xvi*s.*

Beares skinnes the skin red   xvi*s.*

Beares skinnes the skin white   xxx*s.*

Bedelum[6] the pound   xx*d.*

Belles called haukes belles the dosen pair   ii*s.* vi*d.*

---

[1] Bankers were coverings for a bench or chair; verdure was a rich tapestry ornamented with representations of trees and other vegetation.

[2] Basil, sheepskin tanned in bark.

[3] It is not certain what these were. The 1604 Book of Rates has basherons and the 1660 has bashrones. The *O.E.D.* defines bashrones as kettles on the basis of the entry in the 1660 Book of Rates which runs 'Battry Bashrones or Kettles'. This definition seems doubtful, for the 1558, 1562, and 1604 Books have quite separate entries for baserons (or basherons) and kettles; moreover in the 1558, 1562, 1582, and 1590 Books, baserons are valued at 26*s.* 8*d.* cwt., and kettles at 40*s.* cwt.

[4] Bast, any flexible fibrous bark.

[5] Articles of metal, wrought by hammering.

[6] Bdellium, a gum-resin used in medicine.

Belles called horse belles or moris bels course the groce	v*s*.
Belles called sacring belles the groce	xx*s*.
Belles called sacring belles the C containing v.xx pound	l*s*.
Bemovium[1] the pound	xvi*d*.
Benalum[2] the pound	ii*s*. vi*d*.
Benjamin[3] the c. containing v.xx pound	xii*l*. x*s*.
Benjamin the pound	ii*s*. vi*d*.
Benruby[4] the pound	ii*s*.
Bever bellies the peece	viii*d*.
Bever skinnes the role	xx*s*.
Bever skinnes the peece	v*s*.
Bise[5] the pound	viii*s*.
Bisilke[6] the groce containing xii dosen peeces	xiii*s*. iiii*d*.
black Lamb the c. containing v.xx	xxvi*s*. viii*d*.
black Latten[7] rolles the c. containing v.xx xii li.	xxx*s*.
blankets called Paris mantles, red or coloured the peece	xiii*s*. iiii*d*.

---

[1] The 1558 Book of Rates has bemonium and the 1562 has bemonum. It is not clear what it was; the difference in value seems to preclude any identification with benzoin.

[2] Ben-album or behen album (white behen or bladder campion) used in medicine.

[3] Benzoin, a resinous substance obtained from trees growing in the East Indies.

[4] Ben-rubrum or behen rubrum (red behen or sea lavender) used in medicine.

[5] Bice, a pigment which yields a dull blue colour, prepared from smalt.

[6] The cross-reference from Silk (infra, p. 55) implies that this was some sort of real or imitation silk despite the low valuation of just over 1*d*. the piece. It seems impossible to tell what it really was. To identify it with the linen cloth called byssus would not make any better sense (on byssus see E. Baines, *History of the cotton manufacture in Great Britain* (1835), App., pp. 533–43).

[7] Latten-brass, i.e. milled brass in thin plates or sheets, used by braziers and for drawing into wire.

Blankets called Paris Mantles white the peece	x*s*.
Bodkins the M	xiii*s*. iiij*d*.
Bole Armoniack[1] the C containing v.xx xii li.	xx*s*.
Boleus Armenus[2] the pound	xii*d*.
Books unbound the halfe maund	xl*s*.
Books unbound the whole maund xl remes	iiij*l*.
Boords for bookes called paste boordes the M	vi*s*. viii*d*.
Boords for Barrels the M	l*s*.
Boords for shoomakers the peece	xij*d*.
Boras[3] the pound	xiii*s*. iiij*d*.
Bornby[4] the pound	ii*s*.
Bosses for bridles the groce	x*s*.
Bottles of earth covered with wicker the dosen	xx*d*.
Bottles of glasse covered the dozen	xx*s*.
Bottles of glasse covered with lether and with vices the dozen	xxx*s*.
Bottles of Glasse uncovered the dozen	xviii*d*.
Boultel[5] bewpers[6] the dosen peeces	xlviij*s*.
Boultel called raines[7] boultel the dosen peeces	xlviij*s*.
Boultel called raines boultel the peece	iiii*s*.
Boultel the bale containing xx peeces	iiij*l*.
Bowstaves the bundel containing xvj staves	v*s*.
Bowstaves the last containing xxiiiij[8] bundels	vi*l*.
Bowstaves the c containing vi. xx	xl*s*.
Boxes the shock containing lx	xiij*s*. iiij*d*.
Boxes called fire boxes[9] the groce	vj*s*. viij*d*.

---

[1] Apparently the same as Boleus Armenus despite the difference in valuation (Quincy, p. 106).
[2] Bole armeniac, an astringent earth brought from Armenia, used as an antidote and styptic.
[3] Borax.　　[4] Benruby or red behen (supra, p. 8).
[5] A kind of cloth used for bolting or sifting meal or flour.
[6] Probably Beaupreau in France.　　[7] Rennes.
[8] A mistake for xxiiij which is the figure given in the 1558 and 1562 Books of Rates.　　[9] Tinder-boxes.

E

Boxes look more in Navern boxes, Nest boxes, Touch boxes, round boxes, and Sand boxes.

Box peeces for Combes the but, Pipe or fat containing iiij thousand	vi*l.* xiij*s.* iiij*d.*
Box peeces for Combes the thousand	xxxiij*s.* iiij*d.*
Brabant cloth the half peece	xiij*s.* iiij*d.*
Brabant cloth the whole peece	xxvi*s.* viij*d.*
brasel[1] the c. containing v.xx xii li.	xxxiii*s.* iiii*d.*
brasse weights called pile[2] weights the c. containing v.xx xii li.	l*s.*
brewes[3] living the dosen	viii*s.*
brickstones called flaunders tiles to scoure with, the M	xiii*s.* iiii*d.*
brickstones the thousand	vi*s.* viij*d.*
bridle bits the dosen	x*s.*
bridges[4] Thred the dosen pound	xiii*s.* iiii*d.*
brigandines[5] the peece	xiii*s.* iiii*d.*
brimstone the c. containing v.xx xii li.	vi*s.* viii*d.*
bristles the dosen pound	x*s.*
bristles rough the dosen li.	v*s.*
brittain[6] laces the groce	x*s.*
brittish[7] cloth the peece	xx*s.*
brittish cloth the whole peece containing v.xx elles	xxxiii*s.* iiii*d.*
brooches of laten or copper the great groce containing xii small	iij*l.* xii*s.*
Brooches of Latten or copper the small groce containing xii dosen	vi*s.*

---

[1] Brazil, a red wood from which dye was obtained.
[2] A series of weights fitting one within or upon another, so as to form a solid cone or other figure.
[3] Fowls, perhaps a kind of snipe.   [4] Bruges.   [5] Body armour.
[6] Breton.   [7] Breton: the 1558 Book of Rates has Bretishe.

brusels[1] cloth the peece	xx*s*.
brussehs[2] course of heath the dosen	xviij*d*.
brushes fine of heath the dosen	iiij*s*. iiij*d*.
brushes of bear[3] the dosen	iiij*s*. iiij*d*.
brushes called rubbing brusshes of heare the dosen	viij*d*.
brusshes called rubbing brusshes of heath the dosen	vj*d*.
brusshes called wevers brusshes of heare the dosen	ij*s*. vj*d*.
buckram[4] the paper containing iii peeces	xiij*s*. iiij*d*.
buckram the role	ij*s*. vj*d*.
buckrams the dosen roles	xxx*s*.
buckram of french making for hangings the dosen peeces	xxx*s*.
budge[5] black tawed the dosen	xiij*s*. iiij*d*.
budge black untawed the c. contayning v.xx	l*s*.
budge polles the fur containing iiii pains in the fur	xvj*s*. viij*d*.
Budge Naveron[6] the c. legs	vj*s*.
Budge Romney the c. legs	viij*s*.
Budge white tawed the c. contayning v.xx	xx*s*.
Buffe hides[7] the peece	xx*s*.
Bullions[8] for purses the groce	v*s*.
Bumbazins[9] the peece containing xx yardes	xxvj*s*. viij*d*.
Busk cloth[10] brode the c elles containing v.xx	l*s*.

[1] Perhaps Brussels, though the 1558 Book of Rates has Brysell.
[2] *Sic.*   [3] *Sic*, for hear (hair).
[4] A linen cloth.
[5] A kind of fur, consisting of lamb's skin with the wool dressed outwards.
[6] Perhaps Navarra in Spain.   [7] Ox hides.
[8] Knobs or bosses of metal.
[9] Bombasine, a twilled dress-material composed of silk and worsted, cotton and worsted, or worsted alone.
[10] A linen cloth.

Busk cloth narrow, and all manner of cloth in Holland ploy[1] the peece	xxiiii*s*.
Buskins of lether the xij paire	xl*s*.
Bustian[2] the peece	xiij*s*. iiij*d*.
Buttons of thred the great groce containing xxiiij smal groce	ii*s*. vj*d*.
Buttons of silk the great groce contayning xxiiii small groce	x*s*.
Buttons of steel copper tin or latton for Jerkins the groce	xiij*s*. iiij*d*.
Buttons fine damasked woork the dosen	v*s*.

C

Cabiges the C containing v.xx	vi*s*. viij*d*.
Cables or ropes tarred the c. contatning[3] v.xx xii li.	xiii*s*. iiii*d*.
Cables or Ropes untarred the c. containing v.xx xii li.	x*s*.
Caddas look cruel	
Callaber[4] tawed the timber containing xl skins	vi*s*. viii*d*.
Callaber untawed the timber	v*s*.
Callaber seasoned the pane	xvj*s*.
Callaber stage[5] the pane	x*s*.
Calamus[6] the c. containing v.xx	l*s*.
Camerick[7] the peece containing xiii elles english	xl*s*.

---

[1] A ply or fold: 'pli caractéristique du drap préparé pour le transport et la vente (drap faudé)' (G. de Poerck, *La draperie médiévale en Flandre et en Artois*, ii. 154). The 1507 Book of Rates has 'clothe that ys follden lyke Holond clothe' (Gras, p. 699).

[2] A cloth of cotton or cotton and linen.   [3] *Sic.*

[4] Calaber, the fur of some kind of squirrel.   [5] Raw, unseasoned.

[6] Sweet calamus, an eastern aromatic plant, used in medicine.

[7] Cambric, fine white linen (from Cambray in Flanders).

Campher the pound	viii*s.*
Candle plates of Latten of all sortes the dosen	xxx*s.*
Candlesticks small the dozen	iii*s.* iiij*d.*
Candlesticks great the dosen	x*s.*
Candle snuffers the dozen	ii*s.* viii*d.*
candle week[1] the pack containing xxx c.[2]	xiii*l.* vi*s.* viii*d.*
Candle week the C containing v.xx xii li.	xiii*s.* iiii*d.*
Canestones[3] the tun	vi*s.* viii*d.*
Cannes of wood[4] the shock contayning lx cannes	x*s.*
Cantarides[5] the pound	vi*s.* viij*d.*
Canvas the bale or bolte	v*s.*
Canvas called barras[6] the c. elles containing v.xx	xl*s.*
Canvas called Newcastle the c. elles containing v.xx	xxx*s.*
Canvas called Normandy canvas brown the c. elles containing v.xx	l*s.*
Canvas called Normandy canvas whited the c. elles containing v.xx	iij*l.* vj*s.* viij*d.*
Canvas called course packing canvas the c. elles containing v.xx	xxvj*s.* viij*d.*
Canvas quilted with silke the peece	xvj*s.* viij*d.*
Canvas called spruce[7] Canvas the c. elles containing vj.xx	xxvj*s.* viij*d.*
Canvas striped with silk the peece	x*s.*
Canvas striped with thred the peece	vj*s.* viij*d.*

---

[1] Wick.

[2] A mistake for xx c., which is the amount given in the 1558, 1562, and 1590 Books of Rates.

[3] Caen-stone, building stone from Caen in Normandy.

[4] Wooden drinking vessels.

[5] Cantharides, a dried beetle, used in medicine.

[6] Barras, a coarse linen fabric imported from Holland.

[7] Of Prussia.

Canvas called vetery[1] canvas the Bale or fardel
    containing iij c. after v.xx   v*l.*

Canvas called woorking canvas narrowe the c.
    elles containing v.xx   l*s.*

Canvas called woorking canvas el brode the c.
    containing v.xx   iiij*l.* iij*s.* iiij*d.*

Canvas or woorking canvas of the brodest
    sorte the c. containing v.xx elles   v*l.*

Canvas look Packduck and Soulwich

Cap golde the pound   x*s.*

Cap riband the dozen peeces   xxvj*s.* viij*d.*

Caps with single cronnes the dosen   xx*s.*

Caps for Children and night caps the dosen   x*s.*

Caps called pressed caps or prest caps the
    dosen   xxx*s.*

Caps double turfed called cockred caps the
    dosen   xxxiiij*s.*

Caps look more in night caps

Capers the pound   iiij*d.*

Caraway seed the c. containing v.xx xij li.   xx*s.*

Cardes to play on the groce   xx*s.*

Cardes look in wool cardes

Cardiamomum[2] the pound   ij*s.*

Carpe balsamum[3] the pound   ii*s.*

Carpets called gentish[4] carpets the dosen   xxx*s.*

Carpets called Turky carpets of iiii yardes and
    aboove, the peece   vj*l.*

Carpets called Turky carpets under that length,
    the peece   xxvj*s.* viij*d.*

---

[1] Vitry. [2] Cardamon, a spice used in cookery and medicine.
[3] Carpobalsamum, an ingredient of mithridate, made from the berries
of the 'balsam-shrub', which grew in the Levant (Quincy, p. 406; Pomet,
p. 205). [4] Of Ghent.

Carpets called Turkie or Venice carpets the peece	x*s*.
Cartanus[1] the pound	viij*d*.
Cart nailes the sum	vi*s*. viij*d*.
Carving knives the dosen	xx*s*.
Carving knives the stock or case	vi*s*. viij*d*.
Carving tooles the dosen	x*d*.
Cases look in combe cases, needle cases and spectacle cases	
Caskets great the dosen	xxx*s*.
Caskets middle the dosen	xxiiii*s*.
Caskets smal the dosen	xv*s*.
Caskets called steel caskets the dozen	iii*l*.
Cassia fistula[2] the c. containing v.xx li.	x*l*.
Cassia legera[3] the pound	xij*d*.
Castium[4] the pound	ii*s*.
Costorum[5] the pound	xvi*d*.
Castrum[6] the pound	ii*s*. vi*d*.
Cats pouts the mantle	v*s*.
Cats pouts the c. containing v.xx	xiij*s*. iiii*d*.
Cats wombes the pane	v*s*.
Cats skins the c. containing v.xx	xxvj*s*. viij*d*.
caules of linnen for women the dozen	iiii*s*.
Caules of silk for Children the dosen	xiij*s*. iiii*d*.
Ceparons[7] the pound	ii*d*.

---

[1] Carthamus, plants yielding red and yellow dyes.

[2] A laxative derived from a wide variety of trees which produce senna leaves and cassia pods.

[3] Cassia lignea or cassia bark, an inferior form of cinnamon.

[4] Probably cost, a herb (alecost or costmary) used in medicine and to give a flavour to ale.

[5] Castoreum or castor, a substance used in medicine and perfumery, obtained from the beaver. The 1562 Book of Rates has castorium.

[6] Probably some form of castor, despite the different valuation.

[7] The 1558 Book of Rates has ciperus; the plant cyperus, probably sweet cyperus or galingale.

Cern[1] the pound	iij*d*.
Cesterns of Latten for cobards the pound	vj*d*.
Chamlets[2] watered and unwatred the peece	xx*s*.
Chamlets the double peece containing xx yardes	xl*s*.
Chamlets look in grograin and silk Chamlets	
Chafing dishes of latten the dozen	xx*s*.
Chafing dishes of Iron the dosen	vi*s*. viij*d*.
Chaines look in copper and Dog chaines	
Chesse boords the dosen	iiij*s*.
Chesse men the groce	vi*s*.
Chests of spruce or dansk[3] the nest contayning three	xiij*s*. iiij*d*.
Chests look more in Sipers and Iron chests	
Chisels for Joyners half the dosen	ij*s*.
Chisels for Joyners whole the dosen	iiij*s*.
Ciclamen[4] the pound	xij*d*.
Clapholt[5] the great c. containing xxiiij small	vj*l*.
Clapholt the small hundred contayning v.xx	v*s*.
Cllaricordes[6] the pair	vj*s*. viij*d*.
Clokes called felt cloke the peece	xiij*s*. iiij*d*.
Cloth of Calico the peece	vj*s*. viij*d*.
Clothe of Golde plain, the yard	xxvj*s*. viij*d*.
Cloth of Golde wrought the yarde	xl*s*.
Cloth of Silver plain, the yarde	xxvj*s*. viij*d*.
Cloth of silver wrought the yard	xl*s*.
Cloth of tissue the yard	iij*l*. vj*s*. viij*d*.

---

[1] Perhaps some sort of kernel or walnut (from the French *cerneau*?).
[2] Camlet, a mixed fabric of uncertain composition.
[3] Danzig.   [4] The plant cyclamen.
[5] A small size of split oak, for barrel-staves, and wainscoting.
[6] Clavichords.

Cloth called crest cloth the peece containing vi yardes[1]	xl*s*.
Cloth look more in Brabant, brittish, brucels, buske, camerick, henego, florence, Isingham, flemish, french, harnesdale and at linnen cloth	
Cloves the pound	v*s*.
Cloves the c. pound containing v.xx	xxv*l*.
Cocheneli[2] the pound	vj*s*. viij*d*.
Codfish the last containing iiij c.	v*l*.[3]
Codfish the c. containing v.xx	xxx*s*.
Codfish the barrel	x*s*.
Codsheds the barrel	iij*s*. iiij*d*.
Codsheds the last containing xij barrels	xl*s*.
Cofers with iron barres the nest containing three	xvj*s*.
Cofers plain the nest containing three	vj*s*. viij*d*.
Cofers coverd with guilt lether the dozen	xx*s*.
Cofers covered with velvet the dozen	xl*s*.
Cofers look more in painted Cofers	
Colefish[4] the c. containing vj.xx	xx*s*.
Coles the chauldre containing xxxvj bushels common measure and xxiij bushels water measure[5]	vj*s*. viij*d*.
Coliander[6] seed the c. containing v.xx xij li.	xiij*s*. iiij*d*.

---

[1] A mistake for vi.xx yards, which is the amount given in the 1558, 1562, and 1590 Books of Rates.

[2] Cochineal.

[3] A mistake for vj*l*., which is the amount given in the 1558, 1562, and 1590 Books of Rates.

[4] Coal-fish.

[5] Presumably refers to coal imported from Scotland. The measure appears to be the London chaldron of 26 to 27 cwt. (J. U. Nef, *The rise of the British coal industry*, ii. 367–8).

[6] Coriander seeds.

Colloquintida[1] the pound	xij*d*.
Colloquintida the c. containing v.xx	v*l*.
Combe cases garnished with Ivory combes small the dosen	xiij*s*. viij*d*.
Combe cases garnished with Ivory combes middle sorte the dozen	xx*s*.
Combe cases garnished with Ivory combes large the dosen	xl*s*.
Combe cases garnished with wood combes the dosen	x*s*.
Combe cases single the groce	vj*s*. viij*d*.
Combe cases double the groce	xiij*s*. iiij*d*.
Combes the box containing half a groce	v*s*.
Combes the case	xx*s*.
Combes the groce	v*s*.
Combes of horne for barbers the dosen	xij*d*.
Combes look in horse combes	
Comine[2] the c. containing v.xx xij li.	xxvj*s*. viij*d*.
comin the bale containing iii c. after v.xx xij the c.	iiij*l*.
compasses for carpenters or Joyners, the dosen	ij*s*.
compasses for ships the dosen	v*s*.
Confets[3] the pound	xij*d*.
Copper look in brooches and Buckels	
Copperas[4] the pipe or but contayning viij c.	iiij*l*.
Copperas green the c. contayning v.xx xij li.	x*s*.
Copperas white the pound	iiij*d*.

---

[1] Coloquintida or colocynth, the bitter-apple, used as a purgative.
[2] Cumin.
[3] Comfits, sweetmeats made of fruit and sugar.
[4] Protosulphates of copper (blue copperas), iron (green copperas), and zinc (white copperas); used in dyeing, tanning, and making ink.

Copper golde, quilles or roules the li. containing xij unces	xiijs. iiijd.
Copper round or square the c. containing v.xx xii li.	xls.
Copper chaines the groce	iiijs.
Copper brooches look brooches	
Copper rings fine with stones the dosen	iijs. iiiid.
Corall white or red the mast contayning ij li. di.	xxs.
Corans[1] the c. containing v.xx xij li.	xxxs.
Cork made for diers the last contayning xij barrels	iiijl.[2]
Corck made for Dyers the barrel	vs.
cork made for shoomakers the dozen	iiijs.
corck tacks the M	xvjs. viijd.
Cornu Unicornium[3] the unce	xxs.
corslet harnesse the peece	xxs.
Corteos caparis[4] the pound	xijd.
costum[5] the pound	ijs.
Cotten olde for womens heds the elle	xijd.
Cotten new for womens heds the yarde	xxd.
cotten unspun the c. containing v.xx	iijl. vjs. viijd.
cotten spun the c. containing v.xx	vl.
Counters the nest containing three in one	xxvjs. viijd.
counters the peece	ixs.

---

[1] Currants.
[2] A mistake for iijl., which is the figure in the 1558, 1562, and 1590 Books of Rates.
[3] Unicorn's horn; in the powdered form it was used as an antidote against poison.
[4] Cortex capparis, the bark of the shrub producing capers, used as a drug (Quincy, p. 139).
[5] Cost, a herb (alecost or costmary) used in medicine and to give a flavour to ale.

Counters of Latten the pound   xij*d*.[1]
Crest cloth look in cloth
Crippins[2] with silk the dosen   xxvj*s*. viij*d*.
Crippins with golde the dosen   xl*s*.
Crippin partlets[3] with silk the dosen   iiij*l*.
Crippin partlets with golde or silver the dosen   vj*l*.
Crippin sleeves of golde or silver the dosen
    pair   viij*l*.
Crippin sleeves of silk the pair   x*s*.
christall beades the M   xl*s*.
Crosbowe laths the pound   viij*d*.
Crosbowe thred the pound   iiij*d*.
Crosbowe thred the barrel containing v.xx li.   xxxiij*s*. iiij*d*.
Cruel[4] or worsted yarne the dosen pound   xvj*s*. viij*d*.
Cruel, caddas[5] or worsted ribbon the dosen
    peeces   x*s*.
Cruel girdles the groce   xiij*s*. iiij*d*.
Cruses of stone without covers the c. con-
    taining v.xx   v*s*.
Cruses of stone with covers the c. containing
    v.xx   xiij*s*. iiiij*d*.[6]
Cuball[7] the pound   xiiij*d*.
Cullen[8] golde or silver[9] the mast containing ij
    pound and a half   xiij*s*. iiij*d*.

---

[1] A mistake for x*d*., which is the figure in the 1558, 1562, and 1590 Books
of Rates.

[2] Crepine, a net or caul for the hair; part of a hood; a fringe of lace or
network.

[3] Neckerchiefs, collars, or ruffs.

[4] Crewel, a worsted yarn.   [5] Caddis, a worsted yarn.

[6] A mistake for xiij*s*. iiij*d*., which is the figure in the 1558 and 1562 Books
of Rates.

[7] Cubeb, a berry used in medicine and cookery.

[8] Cologne.

[9] Cologne gold or silver was gold or silver thread.

Cullen hemp or other hemp the sack contayning iii c.	iii*l*.
Cullen hemp or other hemp the c. containing v.xx xii li.	xx*s*.
Cullen hemp or other the dosen pound	ii*s*. vi*d*.
Cullen silk the clout containing iiii pound	iii*l*.
Cullen thred the bale	xii*l*.
Curten rings the pound	viii*d*.
Cusshen clothes course the dosen	xxiiii*s*.
Cusshen clothes of Holland making the dosen	xxx*s*.
Cuttle bones the M	xiij*s*. iiij*d*.

D

Daggers course the dosen	xiii*s*. iiii*d*.
Daggers fine for children the dosen	ii*s*.
Daggers of bone for children the groce containing xii dosen	x*s*.
Daggers black with velvet shethes the dosen	xxx*s*.
Daggers with velvet shethes gilt the dosen	xl*s*.
Dagges[1] with fire locks the peece	x*s*.
Dagswaines[2] the peece	ii*s*.
Damaske[3] and carfa[4] damaske the yarde	viij*s*.
Damask or carfa damask crimson or purple in grain[5] the yard	xiii*s*. iiii*d*.
Damask napkins the dosen	xiii*s*. iiii*d*.
Damaske toweling the peece	xl*s*.
Damask table clothes the peece containing xx yardes	iiii*l*. vi*s*. viii*d*.
Damask table clothes the yarde	iii*s*. iiii*d*.

---

[1] Dags, a kind of heavy pistol or hand-gun.
[2] Dagswain, a coarse coverlet of rough shaggy material.
[3] Damask could be either a rich silk or a linen fabric; the damask napkins etc. were obviously linen.
[4] Caffa, a rich silk cloth. [5] Dyed with kermes or scarlet grain.

Damask[1] lether the dosen tawed	xxs.
Dates the c. containing v.xx xij li.	xls.
Deale called Meighborow[2] deale the peece	viiid.
Deale called Meighborow deale the c.	iiil. vis. viiid.
Deale boord great called spruce deale the peece	iis. vid.
Deales called Norway deales the peece	xxd.
Deskes the dosen	xxs.
Deskes the deske	xxd.
Diagredium[3] the pound	vis. viijd.
Dialls of wood the dosen	xijd.
Dialles of bone the dosen	ijs. vjd.
Diaper[4] table clothes the peece contayning xx yardes	xls.
Diaper table clothe the yard	iis.
Diaper toweling the peece	xxxs.
Diaper napkins the dosen	viijs.
Dictanus[5] the pound	vjd.
Dog chaines the groce contayning xij dosen	xxs.
Dogstones[6] the last containing xi[7] paire	vjl.
Dornicum[8] the pound	ijd.
Dornix[9] with caddas the peece contayning xv yardes	xs.

---

[1] The 1558 Book of Rates has 'Danske'.

[2] The identity of this place is uncertain. It has been identified as either Marienburg in Germany or Mebø near Flekkerø in Norway (R. W. K. Hinton, *The port books of Boston, 1601–1640*, p. li n.). Meighborow deals are not found in the Books of Rates before 1582.

[3] Diagrydium, a preparation of scammony, used in pharmacy.

[4] A linen cloth.

[5] Diptamus or dittany, a plant used in medicine.

[6] Stones used for millstones.

[7] A mistake for xij pair, which is the number given in the 1558 and 1562 Books of Rates.

[8] The 1558 and 1562 Books of Rates have doronicum; probably doronicum romanum or wolfsbane, the root of which was used in medicine.

[9] Dornick, cloth originally manufactured at Doornick in Flanders.

Dornix with silk the peece contayning xv
   yardes   xiij*s*. iiij*d*.
Dornix with wool the peece containing xv
   yardes   x*s*.
Dornix with thred the peece containing xv
   yardes   vj*s*. viij*d*.
Dornix called green dornix or Tirentalles,[1] the
   peece containing xxx yardes   xiij*s*. iiij*d*.
Dornix called french dornix the el   xv*d*.
Dornix called french dornix the yarde   xij*d*.
Double iron plates called doubles the shock
   containing vi bundels   xl*s*.
Doubles the bundel containing x in every
   bundel   vj*s*. viij*d*.
Doubles the peece   viij*d*.
Dowlas or lockram[2] the peece contayning v.xx
   elles   xxxiij*s*. iiij*d*.
Dragagantum[3] the pound   xii*d*.
Drinking glasses of the french making the
   dosen   -   viij*d*.
Drinking glasses of Venice making the dosen   iiij*s*.
Doublets of canvas quilted the peece   x*s*.
Doublets of canvas the peece   v*s*.
Doublets of silk quilted the peece   xxvj*s*. viij*d*.
Duckers[4] the timber   vi*s*. viij*d*.
Dudgion[5] the c peeces containining[6] v.xx   x*s*.

---

[1] Perhaps tiretaine, a mixed cloth of wool and linen or cotton (G. de
Poerck, *La draperie médiévale en Flandre et en Artois*, i. 231–2, ii. 199).
[2] Dowlas and lockram were types of linen cloth.
[3] Tragacanth, a gum used in medicine.
[4] Dockerers, apparently fur made of the skin of the weasel.
[5] Dudgeon, a kind of wood used for the handles of knives, daggers, etc.
[6] *Sic.*

E

Eare pickers of bone the groce	v*s.*
Eeles called stub[1] Eeles the barrel	xlvj*s.* viij*d.*
Eeles called stub Eeles the last contayning xii barrels	xxviij*l.*
Eeles called shaft, kine or dole Eeles the barrel	xxx*s.*
The last of either containing xii barrels	xviij*l.*
Eeles called pimper Eeles the last containing xii barrels	xii*l.*
Eeles called pimper Eeles the barrel	xx*s.*
Eeles the cag	iij*s.* iiij*d.*
Eeles called spruce elles[2] the barrel	xl*s.*
Egrits the dosen foules	viij*s.*
Eleborus albus[3] the pound	vi*d.*
Emery stones the c. containing v.xx xii li.	iiii*s.*
Emptie barels small for grocers the dosen	ii*s.*
Epithium[4] the pound	xij*d.*
Erious[5] the c. containing v.xx xii pound	xx*s.*
Earthen pots single the c. containing v.xx without covers	v*s.*
Earthen pots single the c. containing v.xx with covers	xiij*s.* iiii*d.*
Earthen pots the the[6] c cast contayning iii to a cast	x*s.*
Estrige[7] fethers look in Fethers	
Estrige wul the c. containing v.xx xii li.	xvj*s.* viij*d.*
Estridge wul the sack contayning xvi c.	xiii*l.* vi*s.* viii*d.*

---

[1] The meaning of these different sorts of eels seems to be unknown.
[2] *Sic.*   [3] White Hellebore, a drug.
[4] Epithyme, a plant used in medicine.
[5] Ireos or orris-root; the root of the Florentine Iris, used in pharmacy.
[6] *Sic.*   [7] Ostrich.

Esustum[1] the pound	xii*d*.
Euphorbium[2] the pound	viii*d*.
Excelsa balsamum[3] the pound	vi*s*. viii*d*.

F

Fethers called Estridge Fethers the tuft	v*s*.
Fethers called Estridge Fethers undrest the li.	v*s*.
Fethers for beds the c. containing v.xx xij li.	xxx*s*.
Fether beds olde or new the peece	xiij*s*. iiij*d*.
Figs the sorte containing iii peeces	viij*s*.
Figs the peece	ij*s*. viij*d*.
Figs of Algary[4] the peece containing ij li.	viij*d*.
Figs dodes[5] the topnet containing xxx li.	xx*d*.
Figs the c. containing v.xx xij pound	xiii*s*. iiij*d*.
Filings of Iron called Swarf the c. containing v.xx xij li.	iii*s*. iiij*d*.
Fire shovels the dosen	vj*s*. viij*d*.
Fire shovel plates the c. containing v.xx xij li.	xii*s*.
Fish called barreld fish the barrel	x*s*.
Fish called barreld fish the last contayning xii barrels	vj*l*.
Fish of new land[6] the c. containing vi.xx of the great	xxx*s*.
Fish of new land the c. containing vi.xx of the middle	xx*s*.
Fish of new land the c. containing vi.xx of the small	x*s*.

---

[1] Aes ustum or 'burnt copper', used in medicine (Pomet, p. 338).
[2] A gum resin used as an emetic and purgative.
[3] Perhaps a balm or balsam from the Levant, which was later said to be the most excellent (M. Postlethwayt, *The universal dictionary of trade and commerce* (1751), i. 190).
[4] Algarve in Portugal.
[5] Fig-dode, an inferior kind of fig.   [6] Newfoundland.

F

Fish look Barel fish, Codfish, Colefish, Eeles,
  Gulfish, Haddocks, Hering, Lamprey,
  Ling, Lubfish, Salmon, Saltfish, Sealfish,
  Staplefish, Stockfish, and Whiting

Fitches[1] the mantle	x*s*.
Fitches the timber	vi*s*. viij*d*.
Flanel the yarde	viij*d*.
Flaskets[2] for gun poulder covered with lether the dosen	iii*s*. iiij*d*.
Flaskets for gun poulder covered with velvet the dosen	xxvj*s*. viii*d*.
Flaskets of horne the dozen	v*s*.
Flaunders bands[3] the dozen	xiij*s*. iiii*d*.
Flaunders neckerchefs the dozen	xxx*s*.
Flaunders tile look Bricks	
Flax the bale wherof a cxx[4] is a last	xiiij*d*.
Flax the whole pack containing cl bales waying xx c. at v.xx xii li. the c.	viij*l*.
Flax the dosen pound	ii*s*. vi*d*.[5]
Flax wrought the c. containing v.xx xii li.	xx*s*.
Flax unwrought the c. containing v.xx xii li.	xiij*s*. iiii*d*.
Flemish cloth the whole peece	xxvi*s*. viij*d*.
Florence wullen cloth the yarde	v*s*.
Florey[6] the pound	ij*s*.
Foyne[7] backs the dosen	vj*s*. viij*d*.

---

[1] The fur of the polecat.
[2] Small flasks, but the 1558 Book of Rates has simply flasks.
[3] Neck-bands or collars for shirts.
[4] Printed as 'c, xx' in the original, but it must mean 120 and not a hundred score.
[5] A mistake for ii*s*. viij*d*., which is the value given in the 1558, 1562, and 1590 Books of Rates.
[6] A blue pigment consisting of the scum collected from the vat in dyeing with woad or indigo.
[7] Foin, the beech-marten.

Foine tailes the pane	x*s*.
Foyne wombes the pane	xvj*s*.
Foyne wombes stage the pane	x*s*.
Folium[1] the pound	xii*d*.
Fox skinnes the pane or mantle	x*s*.
Fox skinnes the peece	viii*d*.
Fox wombes, poules or peeces the pane	viij*s*.
Frankencence the c. containing v.xx xii li.	xxvi*s*. viij*d*.
French woollen cloth the peece contayning xii yardes	vj*l*.
Frying pannes the c. containing v.xx xii pound	xiij*s*. iiij*d*.
Frisado[2] the whole peece contayning xxiiij yardes	vi*l*.
Frisado the half peece containing xij yardes	iij*l*.
Fustian[3] the bale containing xxij peeces and half	xv*l*.
Fustian the half peece containing xv yardes	vij*s*. vj*d*.
Fustian the whole peece	xv*s*.
Fustian of Naples[4] the peece containing xv yardes	xxx*s*.
Fustian called Jean[5] Fustian the whole peece containing xxx yardes	xiij*s*. iiij*d*.
Fustian called Millan Fustian the whole peece	xx*s*.
Fustick[6] the c. containing v.xx xii li.	x*s*.

G

Galbanum[7] the c. containing v.xx	v*l*.
Galanga major[8] the li.	viij*d*.

[1] The 1604 Book of Rates has Folium Indiae; probably malabathri or malabathrum, an Indian leaf used in medicine (Quincy, pp. 79–80).
[2] Frizado, a fine kind of frieze.   [3] A cloth made of cotton and flax.
[4] A kind of cotton velvet.   [5] Genoa.
[6] Fustic, a wood used for dyeing yellow.
[7] A gum resin used in medicine.
[8] Galingale, an aromatic root used in medicine and cookery.

Galingale the c. contayning v.xx pound	vij*l.* x*s.*
Galley pottes the c. containing v.xx	xx*s.*
Galles[1] the c. containing v.xx xii li.	xxvj*s.* viii*d.*
Garlick the c bunches containing v.xx	xiij*s.* iiij*d.*
Gauntlets the paire	ii*s.*
Generall[2] the c. containing v.xx	l*s.*
Geneum[3] the c. containing v.xx xii li.	xxx*s.*
Gentiana[4] the pound	iiij*d.*
Gentish cloth the peece	xxiiij*s.*
Gimblets for Vintners the dozen	iiii*s.*
Ginger the c li. containing v.xx	vij*l.* x*s.*
Ginger the pound	xviii*d.*
Ginger called green ginger the li.	xij*d.*
Girdles called buf girdles course ungilted the groce	vi*l.* xiij*s.* iiii*d.*
Girdles called buf girdles gilted the groce	x*l.*
Girdles of lether the groce	x*s.*
Girdles of velvet gilted the dosen	iij*l.* vj*s.* viij*d.*
Girdles of velvet ungilt the dozen	xl*s.*
Girdles look more in Cruel and Woollen	
Girth web the groce	vi*s.* viij*d.*
Gitterns[5] the dosen	liij*s.* iiij*d.*
Glasse broken the barrel	iij*s.* iiij*d.*
Glasse coulered Burgon[6] the Chest	l*s.*
Glasse white called Burgon glasse the Chest	xl*s.*
Glasse coulored the case Normandy	xl*s.*
Glasse white called Normandy glasse the case	xx*s.*
Glasse the way or web containing lx bunches	l*s.*

---

[1] Galls, oak-apples or gall-nuts, used in making ink, tanning, medicine, and dyeing.
[2] General, perhaps a ground colour used in painting.
[3] Gentian; the 1558 Book of Rates has gencium.
[4] Gentian, a root used in medicine.
[5] Citherns. [6] Burgundy.

Glasses to look in, peny ware the groce	viij*s.*
Glasses called halfpeny ware the groce	iiij*s.*
Glasses of all sortes aboove the rates of the groce	iij*l.*
Glasses Reinish the way or web containing lx bunches	l*s.*
Glasses, look in looking, drinking and houre glasses	
Glew the c. containing v.xx xij li.	x*s.*
Gloves of Bridges[1] and french the groce	xxiiij*s.*
Gloves of Canaria unwrought the groce	xvj*s.*
Gloves of Spanish making the groce	xlviij*s.*
Gloves of Canaria, Millon or Venice unwrought the dosen	viij*s.*
Gloves of Canaria, Millon and Venice wrought with silk or Silver the dosen	xxx*s.*
Gloves knit of silk the dozen	xx*s.*
Golde of Bridges[2] the mast containing ij li. di.	xvj*s.*
Golde foile the groce	iiij*s.* iiij*d.*
Golde papers[3] the groce	vj*s.* viij*d.*
Golde skinnes the kip containing l skinnes	xx*s.*
Golde look in Cap golde, Copper, Cullen and Venice golde	
Goteskinnes the dosen	xx*s.*
Grain of Portingale[4] called rotta the pound	iij*s.* iiij*d.*
Grain pouder the li.	vj*s.* viij*d.*
Grain of Civil in beries the li.	iij*s.* iiij*d.*[5]

---

[1] Bruges.   [2] Gold of Bruges was gold thread.   [3] Gold foil.

[4] Grain of Portugal, grain powder, and grain of Seville were all probably forms of kermes or alkermes, the scarlet dye obtained from the dried bodies of insects.

[5] A mistake for iij*s.*, which is the figure in the 1558 and 1562 Books of Rates.

Graines[1] the c. containing v.xx pound	iij*l*. vj*s*. viij*d*.
Graines the pound	viij*d*.
Grana pene[2] the pound	iiij*d*.
Gray[3] tawed the timber	x*s*.
Gray untawed the timber	vj*s*. viii*d*.
Grayes skinnes called flying gray the peece	vj*s*. viij*d*.
Grayes skinnes the skin	viij*s*.
Great Raisins the c. containing v.xx xij pound	vj*s*. viij*d*.
Great Raisins the peece	v*s*.
Greens look in Dornix	
Grograin[4] silk the yarde	vj*s*. viij*d*.
Grograin Chamlets[5] the peece	xxvj*s*. viij*d*.
Gulfish[6] the barrel	vi*s*. viii*d*.
Gum apopomack[7] the li.	iij*s*. iiij*d*.
Gum arabeck[8] the c. containing v.xx xii pound	xx*s*.
Gum Armoniack[9] the c. containing v.xx xii li.	vj*l*. xiij*s*. iiii*d*.
Gum ceraphana[10] the pound	xvi*d*.
Gum dragagant[11] the pound	xij*d*.
Gum edere[12] the pound	xii*d*.
Gum elenum[13] the pound	xvj*d*.
Gum imperii[14] the pound	iiij*d*.

---

[1] Guinea grains or malagueta pepper, obtained from West Africa (J. W. Blake, *Europeans in West Africa, 1450–1560*, i. 40).

[2] Grana pini in the 1558 Book of Rates; perhaps nuts of the pine or fir, used in medicine (Quincy, p. 124).

[3] Grey fur, usually the badger.

[4] Grogram, a coarse fabric of silk, of mohair and wool, or of these mixed with silk.

[5] Camlets. [6] The gull-fish or coal-fish.

[7] Gum opopanax, a gum resin used in medicine.

[8] Gum arabic. [9] Gum ammoniac.

[10] Serapinum or Sagapenum, a gum resin used in medicine.

[11] Tragacanth.

[12] The 1604 Book of Rates has Gum Hederae; perhaps a gum obtained from ground ivy. [13] Gum elemi, used in medicine.

[14] The 1558 Book of Rates has Gum Jiniperi; gum-juniper or sandarac.

Gunnes called handgunnes or half hakes the peece	v*s*.
Gunnes look more in Dagges	
Gunpoulder called corn poulder[1] the c. containing v.xx xii li.	xxxiij*s*. iiij*d*.
Gunpoulder called serpentine[2] the c. containing v.xx xii li.	xx*s*.

H

Hadocks the last contayning xii barrels	iiij*l*.
Halberts gilt the peece	vi*s*. viij*d*.
Halberts ungilt the peece	xx*d*.
Hampers[3] the dosen	iij*s*. iiij*d*.
Hampers the nest containing three	iii*s*. iiij*d*.
Handkerchefs the dosen	xx*s*.
Handovers[4] the c. contayning xii.xx elles	iiij*l*.
Hanging locks of the greatest sort the groce	xl*s*.
Hanging locks of the smale sorte the groce	xx*s*.
Harmodacus[5] the pound	xii*d*.
Harnesdale cloth the peece contayning xxx elles	xxiiij*s*.
Harnesse called demilances the peece	xxvi*s*. viij*d*.
Harnes look Almain rivets, Brigandines, Corslets, Gauntlets, Morians, Salets, and Sculles	
Harnes nailes the sum containing xM	x*s*.
Harp strings the box containing xii groce	xvj*s*.

---

[1] Corn powder: gunpowder that has been granulated.
[2] Gunpowder in fine meal as distinguished from the corned or granulated kind.
[3] A mistake for Hammers; the 1558 and 1590 Books of Rates have Hammers. The error seems to have arisen in 1562 when the Book first has Hampers.
[4] A linen cloth.   [5] Hermodactyl, a root used in medicine.

Harp strings the groce	xvj*d*.
Hasbrough[1] cloth brown the c. elles containing v.xx	xl*s*.
Hasbrough white the c. elles contayning v.xx	xl*s*.[2]
Hassors[3] the role containing xv c elles at vj.xx the c.	xiij*l*. vj*s*. viij*d*.
Halstred[4] brown the c. elles contayning v.xx	xxxiij*s*. iiij*d*.
Hat bands course the groce	x*s*.
Hat bands fine the groce	xlviij*s*.
Hats of Sattin the peece	vj*s*. viij*d*.
Hats of silk french making for men or women the dosen	xxx*s*.
Hats called Spanish or Portingale felts the dosen	xiij*s*. iiij*d*.
Hats called Spanish or Venice the dosen	xl*s*.
Hats of velvet the peece	x*s*.
Hats of worsted short thrommed called Bridges[5] hats the dosen	xx*s*.
Hats of wul or worsted beeing thrommed the dosen	xiij*s*. iiij*d*.
Hats look more in bast or strawe hats	
Haukes called Faulcon the hauke	xxvj*s*. viij*d*.
Haukes called Goshaukes the hauke	xx*s*.
Haukes called Jerfaulcons the hauke	xxx*s*.
Haukes called Tassels the hauke	xiij*s*. iiij*d*.
Haukes hoods the groce	xiij*s*. iiij*d*.
Hedlack[6] the c. containing xii.xx elles	xl*s*.
Hemp the c. containing v.xx xii li.	xx*s*.
Hemp the dosen	ii*s*. vj*d*.

---

[1] Linen of Hazebrouck in France.
[2] A mistake for l*s*., which is the value given in the 1558, 1562, and the 1590 Books of Rates.
[3] A linen cloth.   [4] A linen cloth.
[5] Bruges.   [6] A linen cloth.

Hemp the sack containing iii c. weight	iii*l.*
Hemp look Cullen hemp	
Henigo[1] cloth in long ploy the peece	xxiiij*s.*
Hering ful the last containing xii barrels	vj*l.*
Hering shotten[2] the last containing xii barrels	iij*l.*
Hering red the cade containing v.c[3]	viii*s.*
Hering red the last containing xx cades or x thousand[4]	viij*l.*
Hernshewes[5] the dosen	xx*s.*
Heath for Brusshes[6]	vj*s.* viij*d.*
Hilts for Swoords the dosen	xiij*s.* iiij*d.*
Hilts, chapes or lockets for daggers the groce	vi*s.* viij*d.*
Hinderlands[7] the c. containing xii.xx elles	iij*l.*
Holland Cloth[8] the peece	xxiiij*s.*
Hook ends the groce	iiii*s.*
Hookes the groce	viij*s.*
Hony the barrel	xxx*s.*
Hoopes for barrels the M	x*s.*
Hops the c. containing v.xx xii li.	x*s.*
Hops the pocket containing three c.	xxx*s.*
Hops the poke containing iiii c.	xl*s.*
Hops the sack containing vi c.	iii*l.*
Hornes called blowing hornes the dosen	xiii*s.* iiii*d.*
Hornes for lanthornes the M	xx*s.*
Horse combes the dosen	ii*s.*
Hose of silk knit the paire	xxvj*s.* viij*d.*
Houre Glasses the dosen	xx*d.*

---

[1] A linen cloth; on ploy see supra, p. 12 n. 1.
[2] A herring that has spawned.
[3] The 1558 and 1562 Books of Rates give the cade as containing a thousand.
[4] The 1558 and 1562 Books of Rates have 20,000.
[5] Heronsews.
[6] No quantity stated; the 1590 Book of Rates has 'the weight'.
[7] A linen cloth.
[8] A linen cloth from the province of Holland.

Houre glasses of flaunders making the dosen of the finest sorte	vj*s.* viij*d.*
Houre glasses of Venice making the dosen	xx*s.*
Huskins[1] for Flechers the skin	vj*d.*

I

Jasper stones for Beades square the c.	xxx*s.*
Javeling heds the hed	vj*d.*
Javeling staves without heds the peece	vj*d.*
Javeling staves with heds the staf	xij*d.*
Jean Fustian look Fustian	
Jenets[2] black raw the peece	x*s.*
Jennets black seasoned the peece	xiij*s.* iiij*d.*
Jenets gray raw the peece	ij*s.* vj*d.*
Jenets gray seasoned the peece	iij*s.*
Jennets gray raw the timber	v*l.*
Jet the barrel contayning xx li.	iij*l.* vi*s.* viij*d.*
Jet the pound	iii*s.* iiij*d.*
Jewes trumps[3] the groce	x*s.*
Imperling[4] the dosen	x*s.*
Imperlings red the dozen	xiij*s.* iiij*d.*
Inck[5] the c. containing v.xx xii li.	xiii*s.* iiij*d.*
Inck hornes the groce	x*s.*
Inckleroles[6] the dosen peeces	xvi*s.* viii*d.*
Inckle unwrought called white thred single or double the c li.	iij*l.* vj*s.* viii*d.*

---

[1] Huss skins; the skin of the huss or dogfish which was used by fletchers for smoothing and polishing arrows.

[2] The jennet was a small Spanish horse.   [3] Jews' harps.

[4] Smit (ii. 953 n. 4) suggests Yperlins or cloth of Ypres. They may however be identified with the fifteenth-century 'eperling', which was a coverlet (P. Studer, *The port books of Southampton, 1427–1430*, p. 108). The 1507 Book of Rates gives them as Iperlyns (Add. Roll, 16577).

[5] Presumably printers' ink (as in the 1604 Book of Rates).

[6] Inkle, a kind of linen tape, or the thread or yarn from which it is made.

Inckle wrought the dosen pound	xiijs. iiijd.
Ipocestes[1] the pound	vjd.
Iron called Amens[2] Iron the c. contayning v.xx xii li.	vs.
Iron called Amens Iron the tun containing xx c. waight	vl.
Iron backs for Chimneyes the peece	iiijs. iiijd.
Iron bands for Kettles the c. contayning v.xx xii li.	xiijs. iiijd.
Iron Chests great the Chest	iijl. vjs. viiiid.
Iron Chests small and midle the Chest	ls.
Iron called fagot Iron the bundle containing v c.	xxvs.
Iron called fagot Iron the c. containing v.xx xii li.	vs.
Iron called Lukes[3] or Spruce Iron the c. containing v.xx xij li.	vs.
Iron called Lukes or Spruce Iron the tun containing xx c.	vl.
Iron called Spanish Iron the c. containing v.xx xij li.	iiiis.
Iron called Spanish Iron the tun containing xx c. weight	iiiil.
Iron called olde Iron the c. containing v.xx xii li.	vs.
Iron pots the dosen	xs.
Iron wyer the c. containing v.xx xii li.	xxxiiis. iiiid.
Iron look more in doubles and spruce iron	
Isingham cloth[4] the peece	xxiiiis.

---

[1] Hypocistis, the solidified juice of a parasitic plant, used as a tonic and astringent. [2] Almain or German.
[3] Lukes can mean either Lucca or Liège; presumably the latter is meant here. [4] A linen cloth.

Isonglass[1] the pound	ii*d*.
July Malabathot[2] the pound	iiii*s*.
Jumb[3] the pound	vi*d*.
Ivory the pound	v*s*.

K

Key knops the groce	x*s*.
Kettles look Battery	
Kids white the mantel	iiii*s*.
Knives paires called Almaine knives and other course knives the groce beeing xii dosen pair	xxx*s*.
Knives paires called Cullen knives the groce	iii*l*. vj*s*. viij*d*.
Knives paires called french knives course the groce	xxx*s*.
Knives called pen knives the groce	x*s*.
Knives called stocks with knives gilt the dosen	liii*s*. iiii*d*.
Knives called stock knives course ungilt the dosen	xvi*s*. viij*d*.[4]
Knives with velvet shethes course for Children the groce	xxx*s*.
Knives fine with Velvet sheathes the groce	v*l*.
Knives look carving knives	

L

Lace called bone lace the dosen yardes	vi*s*. viij*d*.
Laces the groce	vi*s*. viii*d*.

---

[1] Isinglass.

[2] Probably some form of malabathrum, which was an aromatic leaf or a perfumed ointment prepared from it.

[3] Perhaps jujub, i.e. jujuba or zizipha, a sort of plum growing mainly in Provence, used as an aperient and expectorant (Pomet, pp. 134–5). I am indebted to Mr. R. S. Roberts for this suggestion.

[4] A mistake for xxvi*s*. viij*d*., which is the value given in the 1558, 1562, and 1590 Books of Rates.

Lace called Pirle or Cantlet thred the groce	ii*s*. vi*d*.
Laces look more in brittain laces	
Lamber counterfet Amber beades the pound	v*s*.
Lampraies[1] the peece	xii*d*.
Lapdanum[2] the c pound contayning v.xx	iiij*l*. iii*s*. iiij*d*.
Lapis Armeus[3] the pound	v*s*.
Lapis Calaminaris[4] the c. containing v.xx xii li.	x*s*.
Lapis Ematis[5] the pound	vi*d*.
Lapis Lazaris[6] the pound	iij*s*. iiij*d*.
Latten Basons the c. containing v.xx ii li.	l*s*.
Latten called black Latten roles the c. containing v.xx xii li.	xxx*s*.
Latten shaven[7] the barrel containing vi c. at v.xx xii li. the c.	xii*l*.
Latten Wyre the c. containing v.xx xij pound	xl*s*.
Latten shooing hornes the dosen	iii*s*. iiii*d*.
Lawn fine and course the peece containing vi elles demi english	xxx*s*.
Lead, look white Leade or red	
Leaves of Golde the c. containing v.xx	v*s*.
Lemmons the M	vi*s*. viii*d*.
Lether for Cusshens the dosen	vi*s*. viij*d*.
Lether look Basil lether and skinnes	
Letwis[8] the barrel containing ii c. at v.xx xii li. the c.	xx*s*.
Letwis the but containing v timbers	xxxiij*s*. iiij*d*.
Letwis tawed the timber	vi*s*. viij*d*.
Letwis untawed the timber	v*s*.

---

[1] Lampreys. [2] Ladanum, a gum resin used in medicine.
[3] Lapis Armenus, Armenian stone, a blue carbonate of copper.
[4] Calamine, a zinc ore. [5] Haematite.
[6] Lapis lazuli. All these 'stones' were used medicinally.
[7] Thin sheets of latten, thinner than black latten.
[8] Lettice, a kind of whitish grey fur, sometimes applied to the polecat.

Lewers[1] for haukes the peece	viii*d.*
Liberds[2] the pane of wombes	iiij*l.*
Liberd skinnes the peece	xx*s.*
Liberd look in Lyons	
Licium[3] the pound	vi*d.*
Licoras[4] the bale containing two c. at v.xx xij pound the c.	xx*s.*
Lignum aloes[5] the pound	xx*d.*
Lignum balsamum the li.	ii*s.* vi*d.*
Lignum vite[6] the c. contayning v.xx xii pound	x*s.*
Lince[7] called blew lince the dozen	xv*s.*
Linnen cloth called Brizel[8] cloth the peece	xx*s.*
Linnen cloth look Busk, Calico, Crest, Dowlas or lockram, Gentish, Handover, Halstred, Hasbrough, Hassors, Hedlake, Henego, Holland, Hinderland, Middlegood, Minsters, Oulderons, Ozenbridge, Paduck, Pickling, Poledavies, stitchcloth and at Cloth	
Lings the c. contayning vi.xx	iiii*l.*
Lyons or Liberds quick the peece	xxvi*s.* viij*d.*
Litmouce[9] the barrel containing ii c.	xx*s.*
Litmouce the c. containing v.xx xj li.	x*s.*
Locram look Dowlas	
Locks small the dosen	iii*s.* iiii*d.*
Locks look more in hanging locks	

---

[1] Lures for recalling hawks.
[2] Libards, i.e. leopards.
[3] Lycium, the shrub box-thorn, its fruit, or the juice extracted from it.
[4] Liquorice.
[5] Lign-aloes, an aromatic wood obtained from a Mexican tree; but lign-aloes can also simply mean aloes.
[6] Lignum vitae, wood from the guaiacum tree, used in medicine.
[7] Probably a coarse linen cloth.
[8] Brussels?   [9] Litmus.

Long peper[1] the c. containing v.xx	xxv*l*.
Long peper the pound	v*s*.
Long skein white thred the c. contayning v.xx pound	iij*l*. vi*s*. viij*d*.
Looking glasses of Christall large the dosen	xl*s*.
Looking glasses of Christall small the dosen	xx*s*.
Looking glasses of Steel large the dosen	xiij*s*. iiij*d*.
Looking glasses of Steel small the dosen	vj*s*. viij*d*.
Look more in Glasses	
Lormary[2] the c. contayning v.xx xij li.	x*s*.
Lurgerum enium[3] the pound	iiij*d*.
Luzerns[4] the peece	xl*s*.
Lutes with cases called Cullen lutes the dosen	iij*l*.
Lutes with cases called Venice lutes the dosen	xij*l*.
Lute stringes called Minikins the groce	x*s*.

M

Maces the c. containing v.xx	xxxiij*l*. vi*s*. viij*d*.
Maces the li.	vi*s*. viii*d*.
Madder the bale containing viij c. weight	v*l*. vi*s*. viij*d*.
Madder the c. containing v.xx xij li.	xiij*s*. iiij*d*.
Madder called mul madder[5] the bale containing viij c.	xx*s*.
Madder called mulmadder the c. contayning v.xx xij li.	ij*s*. vj*d*.
Mailes look Andlets	
Manna[6] the pound	xx*s*.

[1] Long pepper was used in medicine.

[2] Lormery, the small ironware produced by lorimers.

[3] The 1558 Book of Rates has Lurgermianum, but that does not seem to help in identifying it; perhaps some sort of drug, or could it be lormery ware of copper or bronze?

[4] Lucerns, the skin or fur of the lynx.

[5] Mull-madder, the lowest of the four qualities of Dutch madder.

[6] The juice of certain sorts of ash trees, used as a purgative.

Marbelers plate the c. containing v.xx xij li.	xxxiij*s*. iiij*d*.
Marebolami[1] the pound	xij*d*.
Mercurie sublime[2] the pound	ij*s*.
Margarite[3] the unce	v*s*.
Marking stones the pound	viij*d*.
Marmelade the pound	viij*d*.
Marterons[4] tawed the timber containing xl skinnes	x*l*.
Marteron gilles the timber	viij*s*.
Masts great the peece	vi*s*. viij*d*.
Masts small the peece	iii*s*. iiii*d*.
Mastick[5] the c. containing v.xx	x*l*.
Matches for Gunners the li.	ii*d*.
Middlegood[6] the c elles containing vj.xx	xxvj*s*. viij*d*.
Millensole[7] the pound	iiii*d*.
Millium sole[8] the pound	iiij*d*.
Milstones the peece	xl*s*.
Minikins look Lute strings	
Miniver the mantle	vj*s*. viij*d*.
Minks untawed the timber	xl*s*.
Minks tawed the timber	liij*s*. iiii*d*.
Minsters[9] the role containing xv c elles at v.xx the c.	xvj*l*. xiij*s*. iiij*d*.
Micha[10] the pound	ij*s*. vi*d*.
Mirtille[11] the pound	j*d*.

[1] Mirabolanes or myrobalan, an astringent plum-like fruit, used medicinally.

[2] Mercury sublimate; it was used internally as a medicine and a poison, and externally as a cosmetic.

[3] Pearl.   [4] Martens.

[5] Mastic, a gum or resin.   [6] A linen cloth.

[7] A corruption of milium solis.

[8] Milium solis: gromwell, a plant used in medicine.

[9] A linen cloth originally imported from Münster.

[10] Probably myrrh, as the 1558 Book of Rates has murha.

[11] Myrtle, probably the berries (as in the 1604 Book of Rates).

Mithridatum[1] the pound	x*s*.
Mockado[2] of Flaunders making the peece	xiij*s*. iiij*d*.
Mormiam[3] the pound	xx*s*.
Morris pikes the dozen	xvj*s*. viij*d*.
Morters and pestels of brasse the dosen	xx*s*.
Moule skinnes the dosen	vj*d*.
Mumma[4] the pound	iiij*d*.
Murrions[5] graven the peece	vj*s*. viij*d*.
Murrion plain the peece	ij*s*. iiij*d*.[6]
Musk called Cods of musk the dozen cods	xxvi*s*. viij*d*.
Musk of Levant the unce	xxx*s*.
Musterd seed the bushel	xx*d*.

N

Nailes called Cart nailes the sum	vi*s*. viij*d*.
Nailes great called hed nailes the barrel	iiij*l*.
Nailes great called hed nailes the half barrel	xl*s*.
Nailes called patten nailes the sum containing x thousand	iiij*s*.
Nailes small the barrel	viij*l*.
Nailes small the half barrel	iiij*l*.
Nailes look in Cork, Harnes nailes, sprigs and Teinterhookes	
Napkins called french napkins the dosen	iiij*s*.
Narde celtice[7] the pound	iij*s*. iiij*d*.
Navern Boxes for combes the Bale	xiij*s*. iiij*d*.

---

[1] Mithridate or mithridatum: a composition in the form of an electuary regarded as a universal antidote against poison and infectious disease.

[2] A mixed fabric of wool and silk, in imitation of velvet.

[3] Probably an error for manna, which has the same value; mormiam is not in the 1558 Book, but appears in 1562.

[4] Mummy, a medicinal preparation of the substance of mummies.

[5] Morion, a kind of helmet, without beaver or visor.

[6] A mistake for iij*s*. iiij*d*., which is the value in the 1558 Book of Rates.

[7] Celtic spikenard, an aromatic balsam used in medicine (Quincy, p. 168).

G

Nest boxes the groce	vj*s*. viij*d*.
Needle cases the groce	vj*s*. viij*d*.
Needles the dosen thousand	xx*s*.
Needles look packneedles	
Neckercheefs look Flaunders neckercheefs	
Nigillum[1] romanum the pound	viij*d*.
Nightcaps of linnen the dozen	iiij*s*.
Nightcaps of satten the dozen	xx*s*.
Nightcaps knit of silk the dozen	xl*s*.
Nightcaps of Velvet the dozen	xxx*s*.
Nightcaps of wollen the dozen	x*s*.
Nitrum[2] the pound	ii*s*.
Nutmegs the c. containing v.xx	xvj*l*. xiij*s*. iiij*d*.
Nutmegs the pound	iij*s*. iiij*d*.
Nuts called small nuts the barrel	v*s*.
Nuts called Walnuts the barrel	iij*s*. iiij*d*.
Nux Indica[3] the pound	xij*d*.
Nux Vomeca[4] the pound	vi*d*.

O

Ocam[5] the c. containing v.xx xii li.	v*s*.
Oyle called Civil[6] oyle the tun	viij*l*.
Oyle de bay[7] the barrel containing c li. at v.xx the c.	xxvj*s*. viii*d*.
Oyle olive the barrel containing xxvij gallons waying ii c. xiiij li.	xxx*s*.
Oyle called sallet[8] oyle the gallon	xx*d*.

---

[1] Nigella, a plant of which the seeds were used for medicinal purposes.
[2] Nitre.
[3] Indian nut: it was the coco-nut (J. Gerarde, *The herball or generall historie of plantes* (1636), pp. 1521–2).
[4] Nux vomica, seed of an East Indian tree, which yields the poison strychnia.
[5] Oakum.
[6] Seville.
[7] Oil made from bay or laurel berries.
[8] Salad.

Oyle de spike[1] the pound	ij*s*. vi*d*.
Oyle called train[2] oyle the tun	v*l*.
Oyle look more in Painters oyle and rape oyle	
Oker[3] the barrel	xiij*s*. iiii*d*.
Olde sheets called packing sheets the dosen	xiij*s*. iiii*d*.
Olenum[4] carmomonia[5] the pound	x*s*.
Olenum carioses[6] the pound	x*s*.
Olenum lentissimum the pound	ij*s*.
Olenum masses[7] the pound	x*s*.
Olenum petoleum[8] the pound	vi*d*.
Olenum spice[9] the pound	vi*d*.
Olibanum[10] the pound	xij*d*.
Oliphants teeth[11] the c pound contayning v.xx xii li.	iii*l*. vi*s*. viij*d*.
Olives the hogshed	liij*s*. iiij*d*.
Onions the barrel	xvj*d*.
Onyons the c bunches contayning v.xx	viij*s*. iiij*d*.
Onyon seed the c. containing v.xx xij li.	xxxiij*s*. iiij*d*.
Opium the pound	iij*s*. iiij*d*.
Oppo balsamum[12] the pound	xx*s*.
Opoponax[13] the pound	xvj*d*.
Orchall[14] the c. containing v.xx xij li.	xx*s*.
Orchall the last waying iii c.	iij*l*.
Orenges the M	vj*s*. viij*d*.

---

[1] Oil of spikenard.
[2] Oil from whales, seals, and various fish, especially cod.
[3] Ochre.
[4] It is not clear why the printed Books of Rates give olenum for oleum.
[5] Perhaps Carmona in Spain, but it may mean oil of cardamom.
[6] Perhaps oil of caraway.   [7] Oil of mace.
[8] Oil of petre or petroleum (Quincy, p. 293).
[9] Oleum spicae or oil of spike.
[10] An aromatic gum resin used in medicine.   [11] Elephants' tusks.
[12] Opobalsamum or balm of Gilead.
[13] Opoponax, a gum resin used in medicine.
[14] Orchil, a dye obtained from lichens.

Origanum[1] the pound	viij*d*.
Ores[2] the c. containing vj.xx	iiij*l*.
Ores the peece	viij*d*.
Ornament[3] the c. containing v.xx xii pound	xvj*s*.
Orpiment[4] the c. containing v.xx xii pound	xx*s*.
Orsdew[5] the xij pound	xiij*s*. iiij*d*.
Os de corde Cervi[6] the pound	x*s*.
Osmunds[7] the last contayning xii barrels	v*l*.
Otter skinnes the peece	ij*s*.
Oulderons[8] the bolt containing xxx yardes	xiij*s*. iiij*d*.
Ounce[9] skinnes the peece	x*s*.
Ozenbridge[10] the c elles contayning v.xx	xxvj*s*. viij*d*.
Ozenbridge single the role contayning xv c elles at v.xx the c.	xx*l*.

P

Pack needles the M	v*s*.
Packthred the c. containing v.xx xij li.	xvj*s*. viij*d*.
Packthred called bottom packthred the c. contayning v.xx xij li.	xvj*s*. viij*d*.[11]
Packthred called bottom packthred the dosen	iiij*s*.
Paduck[12] the c elles contayning vi.xx	xxiiij*s*.

---

[1] A genus of labiates, with aromatic leaves, used in medicine.

[2] Oars.

[3] Probably horn-mercury or calomel, used as a purgative.

[4] Trisulphide of arsenic (yellow arsenic), used as a pigment.

[5] Orsidue, a gold-coloured alloy of copper and zinc, rolled into very thin leaf, and used to ornament toys, etc.

[6] Bone of a stag's heart; it got into medicine 'only through a false Philosophy' (Quincy, p. 171).

[7] Bars of high quality iron.

[8] Oulone, a linen or canvas cloth, perhaps named after Olonne in France (P. Studer, *The port books of Southampton, 1427–1430*, p. 4 n. 1).

[9] Lynx.   [10] Linen of Osnabrück.

[11] A mistake for 33*s*. 4*d*., which is the value given in the 1558 and 1562 Books of Rates.

[12] Padduck, a linen or canvas cloth.

Painted clothes the dozen	xiij*s.* iiij*d.*
Painted cofers the nest containing three in the nest	viii*s.*
Painted papers the groce	iiij*s.*
Painted papers the reme	vi*s.* viii*d.*
Painted trenchers the groce	vj*s.*
Painters or Linsed Oyle the barrel	xxvj*s.* vij*d.*
Pannes look in dripping, Frying and warming pannes	
Pannels[1] the c.	xxxiij*s.* iiij*d.*
Paper the bale contayning x remes	xxvj*s.* vij*d.*
Paper called brown paper the bundle	viij*d.*
Paper called cap paper the reme	ii*s.* viii*d.*
Paper called demy paper the reme	iiij*s.*
Paper the reme contayning xx quires	ii*s.* vi*d.*[2]
Paper royall the reme	vi*s.* viii*d.*
Papers called pressing papers the c leaves	vi*s.* vij*d.*
Parkets the groce	iij*s.* iiij*d.*
Parmacitie[3] the pound	x*s.*
Partesants[4] or Bore[5] speares gilt the dosen	iij*l.*
Partesantes or Bore speares ungilt the dosen	xxvi*s.* vij*d.*
Passemin[6] lace of Cruell the dosen	xiij*s.* iiij*d.*
Passemin lace of Golde or silver the pound contayning xii unces	v*l.*
Passemin lace of Silk the groce contayning xij dosen	xx*s.*
Passemin lace of silk and thred the groce	xij*s.*
Passemin lace of thred called Cantlet of thred the groce contayning xij dosen yardes	ij*s.* vi*d.*

---

[1] Panele, unrefined sugar.
[2] A mistake for ii*s.* vij*d.*, which is the value given in the 1558, 1562, and 1590 Books of Rates.
[3] Spermaceti.   [4] Partisans.   [5] Boar.   [6] Passement.

Passemin lace look pomet lace	
Paving stones of earth the M	xx*s.*
Paving stones called hard stones the peece	iiij*d.*
Peares the barrel	iii*s.* iiii*d.*
Peecing thred the dozen li.	xxvi*s.* viii*d.*
Perles look Seed perles	
Penner[1] and Inckhornes the groce	x*s.*
Penners without Inckhornes the groce	x*s.*
Pennets[2] the pound	xii*d.*
Pepper the c. pound containing v.xx	viij*l.* vi*s.* viij*d.*
Pepper the pound	xx*d.*
Pepper look long peper	
Percers[3] the dosen	iiij*s.*
Perosin[4] the c. containing v.xx xii li.	xiij*s.* iiii*d.*
Peticotes knit of silk the dozen	xii*l.*
Peticotes knit of Wul or Cotten the dosen	xxx*s.*
Pickling[5] the c. contayning xii.xx elles	iii*l.*
Pilo balsamum[6] the pound	xx*s.*
Pine[7] the pound	vj*d.*
Pinnes the dosen M	iii*s.* iiij*d.*
Pinpillowes[8] of cloth for Children the dosen	xx*d.*
Pinpillowes of Velvet or silk the dosen	vi*s.* viij*d.*
Pinsons or Pincers the dosen	ii*s.*
Pipes the bale contayning x groce	xl*s.*
Pipes the groce containing xij dozen	iiii*s.*
Pippins look Appuls	
Piretheum[9] the pound	iii*d.*

---

[1] A case or sheath for pens.
[2] Penide, a piece or stick of barley-sugar.   [3] Piercers.
[4] Perrosin, a resin, apparently the dry resin obtained from pine trees.
[5] A linen cloth.   [6] Probably balm of Gilead.
[7] The edible seeds of the stone-pine or other species.
[8] Pincushions.
[9] Pyrethrum, a plant used in medicine.

Pirled lace called cantelet lace of thred the groce	ii*s*. vi*d*.
Piscatia[1] the pound	vi*d*.
Pitch and tar the last containing xii barrels	xl*s*.
Playing tables[2] the dosen	viij*s*.
Playing tables Flaunders making of wainscot the dosen	xv*s*.
Playing tables fine with brasel and bone the dosen	iij*l*.
Playing tables fine of Damask making the dosen	iiij*l*.
Playing tables of Walnut tree the dosen	xxiiij*s*.
Plaster of Paris the mount contayning xxx c. at v.xx xii li. the c.	xx*s*.
Plane Irons for Carpenters the dosen	xii*d*.
Plate gilt the unce	v*s*.
Plate parcel gilt[3] the unce	iiij*s*. vi*d*.
Plate white the unce	iiij*s*.
Plates[4] white or black double or single the c. containing v.xx xii pound	xiij*s*. iiij*d*.
Plates white the barrel contayning v c. weight	iii*l*. vi*s*. viii*d*.
Points the great groce containing xii small	viij*s*.
Points of thred the great groce containing xii small	x*s*.
Poldavies[5] the bolt containing xxx yardes	xx*s*.
Pomet lace of silk the groce	viii*s*.
Pomegranates the thousand	xli*s*. viij*d*.
Portingale skinnes the dozen	xl*s*.
Pots look Cruses, Erthen pots, Galleypots and Iron pots	

[1] Pistachio or pistachio nut.
[2] Playing-boards (as dice-board or chess-board). [3] Partly gilded.
[4] Apparently plated ware. [5] Poldavis, a coarse canvas.

Pouch rings the groce	xv*s*.
Prages[1] the groce	xvi*s*. viii*d*.
Primmers the groce	xxx*s*.
Prunes the c. containing v.xx xii li.	x*s*.
Pullyes of Iron the groce	l*s*.
Pullyes of wood the groce	viii*s*.[2]
Puppets or Babies for Children the groce	vi*s*. viij*d*.
Purling Wyre the dozen li.	viii*s*.
Pursse Wyer the dozen li.	vj*s*. viii*d*.
Pursses for Children the groce	xv*s*.
Pursses look more in Venice pursses	

Q

Quantum centum frigidorum alias Quatuor semini frigidorum[3] the pound	ii*s*. vi*d*.
Quailes the dosen	iiii*s*.
Quern stones the last contayning xij pair of the greatest sort	xl*s*.
Quern stones of the small sorte the last	xiij*s*. iiij*d*.
Quicksilver the pound	xvi*d*.

---

[1] The meaning of this word is uncertain. *O.E.D.* suggests that it may be the same as prag and may mean a pin, nail or spike, but the value of 26*s*. 8*d*. a gross seems much too high for such an interpretation. The 1507 Book of Rates has the entry 'Knyves called prages' (Add. Roll, 16577); Gras gave this as 'Knyves called prags (?)' (Gras, p. 699), but there seems no doubt that it should read 'prages'. Thus prages were apparently some sort of knives. This view is strengthened by the fact that prages exported from Bristol in 1480 were measured by the dicker (E. M. Carus-Wilson, *The overseas trade of Bristol in the later Middle Ages*, p. 253). The dicker was used as a measure of edged tools; for example, razors were measured by the dicker of 10 (infra, p. 49).

[2] A mistake for 8*s*. 4*d*., which is the value given in the 1558, 1562, and 1590 Books of Rates.

[3] The 'alias Quatuor semini frigidorum' is not in the 1558 and 1562 Books of Rates; its addition does not seem to help in explaining this mysterious product.

Quilts called French Quilts the dosen	xlviii*s*.[1]
Quilts the peece	iiij*s*.
Quilts of Satin or other silk for beds the Quilt	iii*l*. vi*s*. viii*d*.

R

Rackets the peece	viii*d*.
Racks for Crosbowes the peece	v*s*.
Rafters the c. contayning v.xx	xxvi*s*. viii*d*.
Raisins of the Sun[2] the c. contayning v.xx xii li.	xvi*s*. viij*d*.
Raisins look great Raisins and Corance	
Ramels[3] the c. containing v.xx xij li.	x*s*.
Rape oyle the last containing xii barrels	xvj*l*.
Rape oyle the barrel	xxvi*s*. viii*d*.
Rapers[4] black with velvet sheathes the dosen	iiii*l*.
Rapers gilt with Velvet sheathes the dosen	viij*l*.
Rasors the dicker containing x	xii*d*.
Rasors the groce containing xii dickers	xx*s*.
Rattles for Children the groce	x*s*.
Recorders the set or case contayning five pipes	v*s*.
Red hides the dicker contayning ten hides	l*s*.
Red lash[5] the dosen	iij*s*. iiij*d*.
Red lead the c. containing v.xx xij li.	xv*s*.
Reedes or Canes the c. contayning v.xx	iii*s*. iiii*d*.
Reedes or Canes the M	xxiij*s*. iiij*d*.[6]
Regalles[7] the paire	xl*s*.

---

[1] A mistake for lviii*s*., which is the value in the 1558 and 1590 Books of Rates.

[2] Sun-dried raisins.

[3] An inferior sort of unrefined sugar; it may sometimes have meant molasses.   [4] Rapiers.

[5] Lasch, a fine kind of red leather, perhaps morocco.

[6] Presumably a mistake for 33*s*. 4*d*.

[7] Regals, small portable organs.

Rhabarbarum[1] the pound	v*s*.
Rhaponticum[2] the pound	ii*s*.
Ribands look in Cap, Threden and Venice Ribands	
Rice the c. pound containing v.xx xii pound	xvj*s*.
Rie the quarter	v*s*.
Rings look more in Copper, Curten and Pouch rings	
Roan skinnes[3] the dosen	xxx*s*.
Rods great the bundle	xx*d*.
Rods small the bundle	iiii*d*.
Ropes look in Bast ropes and Cables	
Rose Algare[4] the c. contayning v.xx xii pound	xl*s*.
Rosen[5] the peece	iii*s*. iiij*d*.
Roset[6] the pound	vi*d*.
Rose water or other sweet water in Glasses of Venice making or other sweet Oyles in like glasses the dosen	vi*s*. viij*d*.
Round boxes the dosen	xiij*s*. iiij*d*.[7]
Rubarbe the pound	xiij*s*. iiij*d*.
Rubbing brushes look Brushes	

S

Sables the timber of the best containing xl skinnes	lx*l*.
Sables of the second sorte the timber	xxx*l*.
Sables of the wurst the timber	xiij*l*. vi*s*. viii*d*.
Sackcloth of silk the yarde	iij*s*. iiii*d*.

---

[1] Rhubarb-root.   [2] A species of rhubarb.
[3] Some kind of skin or leather (perhaps from Rouen).
[4] Rosalger or realgar, disulphide of arsenic, used as a pigment.
[5] Resin.   [6] A rose-coloured pigment.
[7] A mistake for 12*d*., which is the value given in the 1558, 1562, and 1590 Books of Rates.

Sackcloth white of thred the yarde	xx*d*.
Saddle of steel the saddle	x*s*.
Sayes[1] the peece	xx*s*.
Sayes look in silk sayes	
Saffrone the pound	xiij*s*. iiii*d*.
Sal armoniack[2] the pound	iii*s*. iiij*d*.
Sal gemma[3] the pound	xii*d*.
Sallats[4] the peece	xii*d*.
Sallmon the barrel	xxx*s*.
Salmon the last contayning xii barrels	xviij*l*.
Salmon girles[5] the barrel	xv*s*.
Salmon girles the last containing xii barrels	ix*l*.
Salt bay[6] the bushel	vi*d*.
Salt bay the way containing xl bushels	xx*s*.
Salt white the barrel contayning three bushels	ii*s*.
Salte white the bushel	viij*d*.
Salte white the way contayning xl bushels	xxvi*s*. viij*d*.
Saltpeter the c. containing v.xx xii li.	xxx*s*.
Saltfish the last containing xii barrels	vi*l*.
Salt hides the dicker contayning x hides	iij*l*. vj*s*. viii*d*.
Salt sellers the groce	xvj*s*.
Sandalionis[7] the pound	xii*d*.
Sandboxes[8] the groce	vi*s*. viij*d*.
Sanguis draconis[9] the pound	ii*s*.
Sarcenet[10] called Bolona sarcenet the elle	iij*s*. iiii*d*.

---

[1] A light-weight cloth usually made from worsted and woollen yarn.

[2] Sal-ammoniac (ammonium chloride).

[3] Sal-gem or the 'gem-like salt', chloride of sodium.

[4] Sallets, headpieces.   [5] Grilse, a young salmon.

[6] Salt from Bourgneuf Bay, south of the estuary of the Loire (cf. A. R. Bridbury, *England and the salt trade in the later middle ages*, ch. iv).

[7] The 1558 Book of Rates has Sandali omnes; either sandalwood, or sandal, an ointment made from powdered sandalwood.

[8] Boxes with perforated tops for sprinkling sand as a blotter upon wet ink.

[9] Dragon's blood, a bright red gum or resin.

[10] A fine silk material.

Sarcenet of Florence making the elle	iii*s*. iiii*d*.
Sarcenet called Golde sarcenet the yarde	vi*s*. viij*d*.
Satten of Bridges the yard	ij*s*.
Satten of Bridges counterfet Tincell the yard	vi*s*. viij*d*.
Satten of Cipers[1] the peece	xiii*s*. iiii*d*.
Sattin right Crimson or purple in grain the yarde	xiij*s*. iiii*d*.
Satten out of grain the yarde	ix*s*.
Sattin called Tincel with Golde the yarde	xxvj*s*. viij*d*.
Satten called Turkey satten the yarde	v*s*.
Sawes for Carpenters called hand sawes the dosen	iij*s*. iiij*d*.
Sawes called two hand sawes the dosen	vj*s*. viij*d*.
Sawes called Tenant[2] Sawes the dosen	vi*s*. viij*d*.
Sawes called whip sawes the peece	ij*s*. vj*d*.
Saunders[3] white the pound	xvj*d*.
Saunders yellow the pound	xx*d*.
Saunders stocks the c. contayning v.xx xij pound	iiij*l*.
Scales for scabards[4] the thousande	xxvj*s*. viij*d*.
Scamony[5] Cakes the pound	xiij*s*. iiij*d*.
Sculles the hed peece	viij*d*.
Seale fish the fish	xiij*s*. iiij*d*.
Sebastian[6] the pound	viij*d*.
Seed perle the unce	ij*s*. vj*d*.
Seleus Montium[7] the pound	viij*d*.
Semen ambos[8] the pound	iiij*d*.

---

[1] Cyprus.　　　　　　　　[2] Tenon-saws.
[3] Sandars or sandalwood.
[4] The 1558 Book of Rates has Skales voc' skaberdes.
[5] Scammony, a gum resin, used as a purgative.
[6] Sebesten, a plum-like fruit, or a preparation of it used as medicine.
[7] Seleus is sil or seseli, a plant which seems to have been hartwort, the seeds of which were used in medicine (Quincy, p. 164).
[8] Ameos seeds (bishop's weed) used in medicine (Quincy, p. 133).

Semen cartane[1] the pound   iiij*d.*
Semen cucumeri[2] the pound   ii*d.*
Semen papaver[3] the pound   iiij*d.*
Semonie[4] cakes the li.   xiij*s.* iiij*d.*
Sendale[5] the peece containing xxxvj yardes   xx*s.*
Senie[6] the c. containing v.xx   vij*l.* x*s.*
Seodorica alias Zeodaria[7] the pound   iij*s.* iiij*d.*
Seraphium[8] the pound   xij*d.*
Setions[9] the c pound contayning v.xx xii
    pound   xiij*s.* iiij*d.*
Serusa[10] the pound   ii*d.*
Setwall[11] the c. containing v.xx   xxxiij*l.* vi*s.* viij*d.*
Serves albi[12] the pound   viij*d.*
Shanks[13] the pane or mantle   xiij*s.* iiii*d.*
Shermens sheres new the pair   x*s.*
Sheremens sheres olde the paire   vj*s.* viij*d.*
Sheres for Sempsters the mark contayning two
    dosen   iii*s.* iiij*d.*
Sheres called Taylers sheres the dosen   viij*d.*[14]

---

[1] Carthamus seeds, seeds of the bastard saffron.
[2] Cucumber seeds.   [3] Poppy seeds.
[4] Scammony cakes; it is not given in this form in the 1558, 1562, and 1590 Books of Rates.
[5] Sendal, a fine linen, but it can also mean a silk material.
[6] Senna.
[7] Zedoary, a drug obtained from the root of an Indian plant.
[8] Serapine or sagapenum, a gum resin.
[9] The 1558 Book of Rates has Serios; probably serusa despite the difference in valuation.
[10] Ceruse or white lead, used in medicine for ointments.
[11] Perhaps the drug zedoary, though that was valued at only 3*s.* 4*d.* lb. Setwall also means the plant valerian, the root of which was used in medicine.
[12] Serves can mean either the service tree or its fruit; probably therefore the fruit of the service tree.
[13] A kind of fur obtained from the legs of animals, especially kids, goats or sheep, used for trimming outer garments.
[14] A mistake for viij*s.*, which is the value given in the 1558, 1562, and 1590 Books of Rates.

Sheres for Women called Forcepts the groce	vj*s*. viij*d*.
Sherts for men the dosen	xx*s*.
Sherts of mail the peece	xxvi*s*. viij*d*.
Sheetes look olde sheetes	
Shomack[1] the c. contayning v.xx xii pound	xiij*s*. iiij*d*.
Shooing hornes look in Latten shooing hornes	
Showlers[2] the dosen	xvj*s*.
Shuttles for wevers the dozen	ii*s*.
Siles montium[3] the pound	viij*d*.
Silk called Bridges silk the pound	xv*s*.
Silk called Call[4] silk the paper contayning two pound	xxv*s*.
Silk called Floret[5] silk the pound contayning xvi unces	viij*s*. iiij*d*.
Silk of Granado black the pound containing xvi unces	xx*s*.
Silk of Granado couloured the pound contayning xvi unces	xxvi*s*. viij*d*.
Silk long undyed the pound contayning xxi unces	xiij*s*. iiij*d*.
Silk called Nobs of silk the pound containing xxi unces	viij*d*.
Silk called Paris silk the pound containing xvi unces	vi*s*. viij*d*.
Silk raw and dyed the pound contayning xvj unces	vj*s*. viij*d*.
Silk short xxj unces the pound	v*s*.

---

[1] Sumach, a vegetable preparation used in tanning, dyeing, and medicinally as an astringent.

[2] The 1558 Book of Rates has Shovelers. The shoveller was a game bird (shovelard or spoonbill), but perhaps shovels is meant.

[3] Seleus montium (supra, p. 52).

[4] Silk for making cauls ?

[5] Ferret or floss-silk, the rough silk broken off in the winding of cocoons (the 1558 Book of Rates has feret).

Silk called spanish silk the pound contayning xij unces	xxvj*s*. viij*d*.[1]
Silk called satten or spanish silk the li. containing xvj unces	xx*s*.
Silk throwne undyed the pound contayning xvi unces	xiij*s*. iiij*d*.
Silk thrum undyed the pound contayning xvi unces	xiij*s*. iii*d*.
Silk thrum the pound contayning xvi unces	xv*s*.
Silk look in Bysilk and Cullen	
Silk Chamblets the yard	iiij*s*.
Silk sayes the yarde	vi*s*. viii*d*.
Silo balsamum alias Pilobalsamum[2] the pound	xii*d*.
Silver of Brugis[3] the mast contayning ii li. di.	xiij*s*. iiii*d*.
Sinamon[4] the c. containing v.xx li.	xx*l*.
Sinamon the pound	iiij*s*.
Sipers[5] Chests the nest	iiij*l*.
Sipers[6] Cotten the dozen yardes	iiij*s*.
Sirca cola[7] the pound	xii*d*.
Sirop[8] the pound	iiii*d*.
Sissors the groce	xvj*s*. viij*d*.
Sivet[9] called Algare the unce	xxx*s*.
Skinnes called Burdeaux skinnes the dosen	xii*s*.
Skinnes called Dansk skinnes the dosen tawed	xxvj*s*. viij*d*.
Skinnes called Foyne tayles the pane	x*s*.
Skinnes called squirrels skinnes the timber	ij*s*. vj*d*.

---

[1] A mistake for 20*s*., which is the value given in the 1558, 1562, and 1590 Books of Rates.

[2] The 1558 Book of Rates has alias Xilobalsomum, which makes better sense as pilobalsamum is elsewhere valued at 20*s*. lb. Xylobalsamum was the wood of the balsam-shrub (Pomet, p. 205).

[3] Silver thread.   [4] Cinnamon.

[5] Cypress.   [6] Cyprus.

[7] Sarcocollae or Sarcocol, a gum used in medicine (Quincy, p. 125).

[8] Syrup.   [9] Civet.

Skinnes for Furres look Armines, badger,
    Bere, Bever, black Lamb, budge, Calaber,
    Cats, Duckers, Fitchers, Foyne, Fox,
    Gray, Jenets, Kidskins, Letwis, liberds,
    Luzarns, Marterons, Miniver, Minks,
    Moule, Otter, Ounce, Sables, Shanks,
    Wesel, and Wulf

Skinnes for Lether, look Basil, Buffe
    for Cushins portingale, Redhides, Roan,
    Salt, spanish, Spruce and Swan skinnes

Sleeves of Velvet or sattin for Women the paire	x*s*.
Sleeves for Women wrought with silk Golde or silver the paire	xl*s*.
Slip[1] the barrel	iij*s*. iiij*d*.
Smaces[2] the pound	viij*d*.
Snicy[3] the pound	iij*s*. iiij*d*.
Snuffers look Candle snuffers	
Sope called flemish sope the barrel	xiij*s*. iiij*d*.
Sope called flemish sope the last contayning xij barrels	viij*l*.
Sope called Venice or Castle[4] sope the c. containing v.xx xij li.	xv*s*.
Soultwitch[5] the c elles contayning vi.xx	xl*s*.
Spanish skinnes the dozen	iij*l*.
Sparres the c. contayning v.xx	xx*s*.
Speares with heds the c. contayning v.xx	iij*l*.[6]

---

[1] Clay for pottery.

[2] It might mean mace, except that mace was valued at 6*s*. 8*d*. lb. The 1558 Book of Rates has simaces.

[3] Probably a variant of stinice (infra, p. 58).   [4] Castile.

[5] Soultwich, a linen cloth, probably from Salzwedel in Germany (Smit, ii. 982 n. 2.).

[6] A mistake for iiij*l*., which is the figure given in the 1558, 1562, and 1590 Books of Rates.

Speares without heds the c. contayning v.xx	xlvi*s*. viij*d*.
Spectacles the groce	x*s*.
Spectacle cases gilt the groce	xiij*s*. iiij*d*.
Spectacle cases ungilt the groce	vi*s*. viij*d*.
Spica celtica[1] the pound	xvj*d*.
Spicknard[2] the c. contayning v.xx	xxxiij*l*. vj*s*. viij*d*.
Spodium[3] the pound	viij*d*.
Spoones of Alcumine[4] the groce	xvi*s*. viii*d*.
Sprigs the sum containing x thousand	iiij*s*. iiij*d*.
Spruce skinnes for hose the dosen	xxvj*s*. viij*d*.
Spruce Iron the c. contayning v.xx xii pound	xxvj*s*. viii*d*.
Spunges the pound	ii*s*.
Spurres black with Velvet the paire	xx*d*.
Spurres gilt with Velvet the paire	v*s*.
Squilla[5] the pound	ii*d*.
Squinantium[6] the pound	xx*d*.
Squirts the dosen	iiij*s*.
Standishes[7] the dosen	vj*s*.
Standishes covered with lether gilt the peece	iij*s*. iiij*d*.
Staplefish the c. contayning v.xx fishes	xxx*s*.
Starch the c. contayning v.xx xii li.	xiij*s*. iiij*d*.
Staves acre[8] the c pound contayning v.xx	xxxiij*s*. iiij*d*.
Steachas arabia[9] the pound	viii*d*.

---

[1] Celtic spikenard, a root used in medicine (Pomet, p. 119).

[2] Spikenard, an aromatic substance obtained from an Eastern plant.

[3] A fine powder obtained from various substances by calcination; probably some form of tutty (Quincy, p. 108).

[4] Alcamyne or Alchemy, a metallic composition imitating gold.

[5] Squill, the sea-onion, used in medicine.

[6] Squinant or Schoenanth, a sweet-scented grass of Asia, used in medicine.

[7] A stand containing ink, pens and other writing materials.

[8] Stavesacre, a plant, the seeds of which were used as an emetic.

[9] Arabian stechados, a fragrant spice used in medicine; it was improperly called Arabian, being actually found in France and Spain (Pomet, pp. 115–16); probably French lavender.

H

58   A TUDOR BOOK OF RATES

Steele the half barrel contayning l bundles
every bundle vi sheves and every sheaf
xxx gads   vi*l.*

Sticados[1] the pound   viii*d.*

Stinice[2] the pound   iij*s.* iiij*d.*

Sinerci[3] the pound   iii*s.* iiij*d.*

Stirrops the dosen paire   vi*s.*

Stitched cloth to woork on the elle   xx*d.*

Stockfish[4] called Croplings[5] the c. contayning
vi.xx   xiii*s.* iiii*d.*

Stockfish called Croplings the last contayning
x hundred fishes   vi*l.* xiij*s.* iiii*d.*

Stockfish called Titlings[6] the c. containing
vi.xx   vi*s.* viii*d.*

Stockfish called Titlings the last containing x.c iii*l.* vi*s.* viii*d.*

Stockfish called Lubfish[7] the last containing
x.c   xiii*l.* vi*s.* viii*d.*

Stockfish called Lubfish the c. contayning
vi.xx   xxvi*s.* viii*d.*

Stooles called close Chamber stooles with
basons the dosen   iii*l.*

Stooles called close Chamber stooles without
Basons the dosen   xxx*s.*

Stooles called matted stoole the dozen   ii*s.*

Stones look Cane, Dog, Emery, Marking, Mil,
Paving stonnes and Quern stones

---

[1] Stechados or French lavender.
[2] The 1558 Book of Rates has scinci; scinci or skinks were small lizards used in medicine.
[3] Probably a variant of scinci; it is not in the 1558 and 1562 Books of Rates.
[4] Stock-fish, a name for cod and other gadoid fish cured without salt by splitting open and drying hard in the air.
[5] An inferior kind of stock-fish.
[6] A small size of stock-fish.
[7] Lobfish, a kind of stock-fish.

Storax calamit[1] the pound	iiij*s*.
Storax liquid[2] the c. containing v.xx	v*l*.
Storkes the dosen	xx*s*.
Strawhats look in Bast or strawe Hats	
Sturgeon the barrel	liij*s*. iiii*d*.
Sturgeon the firkin	xiii*s*. iiii*d*.
Succado[3] the pound	xi*d*.
Sugar the c. contayning v.xx xii li.	iii*l*. vj*s*. viii*d*.
Sugar the Chest containing iii c	x*l*.
Sugar Candy the half chest the C contayning	
v.xx xii pound	iij*l*. vi*s*. viij*d*.
sumach[4] the c. containing v.xx xii li.	xiii*s*. iiii*d*.
Sulphur vivum[5] the pound	viij*d*.
Swannes the swan	iiii*s*.
Swanquilles the M	vi*s*. viij*d*.
Swan skinnes the skin	ii*s*. iiij*d*.[6]
Swoord blades course the dosen	xiii*s*. iiij*d*.
Swoord blades of sclavony[7] the dosen	xl*s*.

T

Tablemen[8] the groce	viii*s*.
Tables look playing Tables and writing tables.	
Taffata the yarde	vi*s*. viii*d*.
Taffata called Levant Taffata the yarde	xx*d*.
Taffata narrow called spanish Taffata the yarde	iiii*s*.

---

[1] A gum resin in its hard form (Quincy, p. 119).

[2] Balsam of the tree liquidambar orientale, used in medicine.

[3] Succade, fruit preserved in sugar, either candied or in syrup.

[4] A vegetable preparation used in tanning, dyeing, and medicinally as an astringent.

[5] Native or virgin sulphur.

[6] A mistake for 2*s*. 6*d*., which is the value given in the 1558, 1562, and 1500 Books of Rates.

[7] Slavonia.

[8] Men or pieces used in any game played on a board, especially backgammon.

Taffata called Towers[1] Taffata the yarde	iiis. iiijd.
Taylers sheres look sheres	
Tankerds look in Cannes	
Taniorindi[2] the pound	viijd.
Tappistry with Caddas the elle flemish	iis.
Tappestry with Golde called Arras the flemish elle	xls.
Tappestry with silk the flemish elle	iijs. iiiid.
Tappestry of Heare course the flemish elle	viiid.
Tappistry with wul or Verdure the flemish elle	xiid.
Tapsia[3] the pound	xijd.
Targets course the peece	vis. viijd.
Targets fine the peece	xxs.
Tartora[4] the pound	xiid.
Tartornes[5] the post containing xl short peeces	vil.
Tasels[6] the pipe	iiijl.
Tasels the M	vis. viijd.
Taveling[7] the c.	xiijs. iiiid.
Teinterhookes the M	iis. vjd.
Terra bethemia veter[8] the pound	xiid.
Terra bethemia comitis the pound	id.
Terra sigillata[9] the pound	xiid.

---

[1] Perhaps Tours in France.

[2] The 1558 Book of Rates has tamorindi; perhaps tamarindi or tamarinds, an Indian fruit used in medicine (Quincy, p. 182).

[3] Thapsia, a plant used in medicine.

[4] The meaning is uncertain, perhaps tartar.

[5] Tartarines, rich stuff, apparently of silk, imported from the East.

[6] Teazles.

[7] Tavelin, small packages of skins or portions of fur put up between two boards.

[8] The 1558 Book of Rates has Terre bithina veter. Probably Terebinthina Veneta or Venice turpentine; the Terra bethemia comitis was probably terebinthina communis or common turpentine. Both these forms of turpentine were used in medicine (Pomet, pp. 209–10). I am indebted to Mr. R. S. Roberts for this suggestion.

[9] An astringent bole, used as a medicine and antidote.

Thred called bottom thred the c. containing v.xx pound	xxxiii*s*. iiii*d*.
Thred called bottom thred the dosen pound	iiij*s*.
Thred called Lions thred the but	ii*s*.
Thred called Outnall[1] thred the dosen pound	xiii*s*. iiii*d*.
Thred called paris thred the bale contayning c bolts	x*l*.
Thred called paris thred the but	ij*s*.
Thred called Sisters[2] thred the li.	v*s*.
Thred look Bridges thred, Crosbowe thred, Cullen thred, long skein thred, packthred and peecing thred	
Threden ribond the dosen peeces	vi*s*. viii*d*.
Thimbles the M	xiii*s*. iiij*d*.
Ticks[3] called Brussel ticks the Tick	xiij*s*. iiij*d*.
Ticks called Turney[4] ticks for beds the dosen	iiij*l*.
Tin foile the groce	iiij*s*.[5]
Tin glasse[6] the c. contayning v.xx xij pound	l*s*.
Tips for hornes of horne the M	v*s*.
Tongs for fire the dosen	vj*s*.
Tooth picks the groce	xx*d*.
Torbith[7] the pound	x*s*.
Tormarith[8] the c. contayning v.xx xii pound	iij*l*. vj*s*. viij*d*.
Touchboxes covered with Velvet the dosen	viii*s*.
Touchboxes of lether the dosen	xiiij*d*.

---

[1] A linen thread, perhaps from Oudenarde (the 1558 Book of Rates has Owtnarde).

[2] The meaning is uncertain; perhaps from sister, the female member of a religious order, society or gild.

[3] Linen bed coverings.   [4] Tournay?

[5] A mistake for iij*s*., which is the figure given in the 1558, 1562, and 1590 Books of Rates.

[6] Bismuth.   [7] Turpeth or turbith, a cathartic drug.

[8] Turmeric, the aromatic and pungent root-stock of an East Indian plant, used as a dye and medicinally.

Touchboxes of Iron or other mettall gilt the dosen	x*s*.
Towe the c. contayning v.xx xii pound	vi*s*. viij*d*.
Trayes the shock contayning lx	x*s*.
Treacle[1] of Flaunders the barrel	xl*s*.
Treacle of Jean the pound	viij*d*.
Trenchers of common sorte the thousand	v*s*.
Trenchers thick the groce contayning xij dosen	iiij*s*. iiij*d*.
Trenchers look painted trenchers	
Trochestore de vipianum[2] the pound	vj*s*. viij*d*.
Troy weights the dosen li.	x*s*.
Truncks[3] the dosen	xii*s*.
Tukes[4] the peece	viij*s*.
Turky satten look Satten	
Turnsale[5] the c pound contayning v.xx	iij*l*. vi*s*. viij*d*.
Turpentine the c. containing v.xx xii pound	x*s*.
Turpentine look Venice turpentine	
Tutia[6] the pound	iiij*d*.

U

Varnish the c li. contayning v.xx xii li.	xxxiij*s*. iiij*d*.
Velvet right crimson or purple in grain the yard	xxv*s*.
Velvet of all collours out of grain the yarde	xv*s*.

---

[1] Not the syrup obtained from sugar, but a medicinal compound used as a salve.

[2] Troches or lozenges of vipers, used as a drug; the chief ingredient was boiled flesh of the viper (Quincy, p. 418).

[3] Probably hollow tubes from which darts or pellets were shot; the 1604 Book of Rates has 'Trunkes to shoote with'.

[4] A canvas or linen cloth.

[5] Turnsole, a violet-blue or purple colouring matter.

[6] Tutty, a crude oxide of zinc, used in ointments and lotions.

Venecreke[1] the c. contayning v.xx xii pound	xiij*s*. iiij*d*.
venice golde or silver[2] the pound containing xii unces	liij*s*. iiij*d*.
venice Pursses of lether the dozen	xii*s*.
venice pursses of leather imbrodered the dozen	xx*s*.
venice Pursses of silk imbrodered or knit the dosen	xl*s*.
Venice Riband the dosen peeces[3]	xxvj*s*. viij*d*.
venice Turpentine the pound	xx*d*.
Verdegrece[4] the c pound contayning v.xx xii pound	iij*l*. vj*s*. viij*d*.
Verditor[5] the c pound contayning v.xx xii pound	xiij*s*. iiii*d*.
vermillion[6] the c. containing v.xx pound	vj*l*.
vernix alias Sandrar or gratia dei[7] the pound	viii*d*.
vinagre the tun	xlvi*s*. viij*d*.
viols the peece	vi*s*. viij*d*.
virginals double the pair	xxxiiij*s*. iiij*d*.
virginals single the pair	xvi*s*. viij*d*.
Visers the dosen	xii*s*.
viter[8] the pound	xii*d*.
vitolum[9] the pound	ii*d*.

---

[1] Fenugreek, a leguminous plant cultivated for its seeds, which were used in cataplasms and clysters.

[2] Gold or silver thread.

[3] The 1558 Book of Rates has 'the pound', which seems an error.

[4] Verdigris, used medicinally for man and beast.

[5] Verditer, a pigment of a green, bluish green, or light blue colour.

[6] Vermilion, a scarlet pigment.

[7] The 1558 and 1562 Books of Rates have 'sandrake', presumably sandarac, a resin used in the preparation of spirit varnish; gratia dei is the hedge hyssop, and it can also mean a kind of plaster. The meaning here is not clear.

[8] Vitex, a plant; apparently agnus castus (Pomet, p. 13).

[9] Probably vitriol (the 1604 Book of Rates has vitriolum Romanum).

W

Wainescot the c. containing v.xx	iiij*l*.
Warming pannes or bed pannes the dosen	xxx*s*.
Washing balles the groce	xx*s*.
Wax the c pound containing v.xx xii pound	iij*l*.
Weights look in Brasse weights and Troy weights	
Wheat the quarter	vi*s*. viij*d*.
Whetstones the c. by taile	viij*s*. iiii*d*.
Whipcorde the shock containing lx bundles called merline the pound	ii*d*.
Wesel skinnes the dosen	iiij*d*.
Whistling bellowes the groce	xij*s*.
White lead or red the c. contayning v.xx xii pound	xv*s*.
Whitings the last containing xii barrels	xl*s*.
Wine called Renish wine the Awme[1]	x*s*.
Wines of all sortes the tun to be rated from time to time at our pleasure	
Wire for Claricordes the li.	xij*d*.
Wire look Iron wire, Latten wier, purling wire and purse wier	
Wod[2] called Tholos[3] wod the ballet containing ij c.	xxvi*s*. viij*d*.
Wod called Tholos wod the c. contayning v.xx xii li.	xiij*s*. iiij*d*.
Wod called green wod the c. contayning v.xx xii pound	x*s*.

---

[1] Awm or aam, a liquid measure, apparently of 40 gallons (*H.M.C. Salisbury*, x. 245).
[2] Woad.
[3] Toulouse.

Wodmall[1] the peece	xx*s*.
Wolves living the woulf	x*s*.
Wolves skinnes tawed the skin	xx*s*.
Wolves skins untawed the skin	xviij*s*. viij*d*.
Woormseed[2] the c. containing v.xx	x*l*.
Worsted called S. Thomas[3] Worsted narrow or half worsted the peece	x*s*.
Worsted called Russels[4] worsted or brode worsted the peece	xx*s*.
Worsted yarne the dosen pound	xvi*s*. viij*d*.
Wrests for Virginals the groce	xii*s*.
Writing tables the dosen	viij*s*.
Wul called spanish wul the c.	v*l*.
Wul look Cotten and Estridge	
Wul cardes new the dosen	x*s*.
Wul cardes olde the dosen	vi*s*.
Wullen Girdles the dosen[5]	viij*s*.

Y

Yarne called Muscovia or Spruce yarne the c. contayning v.xx xii pound	xxvi*s*. viij*d*.
Yarne called worsted yarne, Cruel or Mockado ends the dosen pound	xvi*s*. viij*d*.

Heer endeth the Rates inwards

---

1 Wadmal, a kind of woollen cloth.
2 Wormseed, a drug used as an anthelmintic.
3 St. Omer.
4 Perhaps from Rijssel, the Flemish name of Lille.
5 The 1558 Book of Rates has 8*s*. the girdle, and the 1562 Book has 8*s*. the gross; 8*s*. the dozen seems to be the correct valuation.

Rates for the subsidie or poundage outwards.

A

Alablaster the lode contayning xv foote square	xxvi*s*. viii*d*.
Ashes english the last contayning xii barrels	x*s*.

B

Bacon the flitch	iiii*s*.
Bagges the dosen	vi*s*. viii*d*.
Beef the barrel	xx*s*.
Bel metall[1] the c. containing v.xx xii pound	xxxiij*s*. iiij*d*.
Beer eger[2] the tun	xiii*s*. iiij*d*.
Beer the tun	xxx*s*.
Bookes look printed bookes	
Butter corrupt the barrel[3]	
Butter good the barrel	xxx*s*.

C

Candels the dosen pound	iiij*s*.
Candels the barrel contayning x dosen pound	xl*s*.
Caps unbottoned[4] English the dosen	xvj*s*. viij*d*.
Calfskinnes the dosen	x*s*.
Cheese called Essex cheese the wey containing xvj.xx and xvj li.	xxvi*s*. viij*d*.
Cheese called Suffolk cheese the wey containing xii.xx xij li.	xxvi*s*. viij*d*.
Cottons[5] the c goades containing v.xx	iij*l*. vj*s*. viij*d*.

---

[1] Bell-metal, an alloy of copper and tin.
[2] Beeregar, sour beer or vinegar made from beer.
[3] No value given; the 1558 Book of Rates gives it as 30*s*.
[4] The 1558 and 1562 Books of Rates have buttoned.
[5] A woollen cloth; the goad was a cloth measure of 1½ yards.

Cunny[1] skinnes black the c contayning v.xx	l*s*.
Cunny skinnes gray the c seasoned containing v.xx	vi*s*.
Cunny skinnes gray stage the c contayning v.xx	ii*s*. vi*d*.

E

Earth, look Red earth

F

Flocks the c. containing v.xx xii pound	xiij*s*. iiij*d*.
Frise[2] the peece	xx*s*.

G

Glovers clippings the maund or fat	xxx*s*.
Goose quilles the thousand	xii*d*.

H

Heath look red Heath	
Hornes rough the M	xxx*s*.
Horse collers of lether the c contayning v.xx	xxvi*s*.
Horse tailes the c containing v.xx	x*s*.
Hose long the pair	iij*s*. iiij*d*.
Hose short the dosen pair	viij*s*.

I

Iron the tun containing xx c weight	viij*l*.
Iron wrought the c. containing v.xx xii pound	xvj*s*. viij*d*.

K

Kid skinnes or broken felles[3] the c containing v.xx	x*s*.

---

[1] Coney.   [2] Frieze, a coarse woollen cloth.
[3] Broke-fells, inferior sheep skins.

L

Lamb skinnes black the c contayning v.xx	xvi*s.* viij*d.*
Lamb skinnes white the c contayning v.xx	xvi*s.* viij*d.*
Lamb skinnes called Morkins[1] the c contayning v.xx	vi*s.* viii*d.*
Lead uncast the foulder containing xix c. di. every c waying v.xx xii pound	viij*l.*
Lead cast the foulder	ix*l.*
Linen shreds called Rags the maund or fat	xxvi*s.* viij*d.*

M

Malte the quarter	vi*s.* viii*d.*
Malt mustie the quarter[2]	
Malvasie[3] the but	vi*l.*
Mantels called Irish mantles the pair[4]	v*s.*
Meale the quarter	xiii*s.* iiii*d.*
Meale the last beeing x quarters	vi*l.* xiii*s.* iiij*d.*

O

Oker look red Oker	
Olde shoos the c dosen	xxxiii*s.* iiii*d.*
Otmeale the barrel	v*s.* iiii*d.*
Otmeale the bushel	xvi*d.*
Otter skinnes raw the peece	xii*d.*
Otter skinnes tawed the peece	xvi*d.*
Otter wombs the mantle	x*s.*

P

Printed[5] bookes the fat	iiij*l.*

---

[1] Morkin, a beast that has died by disease or accident.
[2] No value given; the 1558 Book of Rates gives it as 6*s.* 8*d.*
[3] Malvoisie or malmsey.
[4] The 1558 Book of Rates has 'the pece'.
[5] The 1558 Book of Rates has 'paynted'.

R

Red earth[1] the c. contayning v.xx xii pound	ii*s*. vi*d*.
Red Heath[2] the c. contayning v.xx xii pound	ii*s*. vi*d*.
Red heath the M	xiii*s*. iiij*d*.
Red Oker the hogshed	xx*s*.
Ropes the c. contayning v.xx xii pound	xvi*s*. viii*d*.

S

Sheepskinnes tawed the c. containing v.xx	liii*s*. iiii*d*.
Sheepskinnes untawed called Pelts the c. containing v.xx	xiii*s*. iiii*d*.
Shooes new shooes the c paire	v*l*.
Shooes look old shooes	
Skinnes look Calves, Cunny, Kid, Lamb, Otter skinnes and Otter wombs	
Shreds and lists the barrel	xxx*s*.
Shreds and lists the pipe	iij*l*.
Scarlet the yarde	xvi*s*. viij*d*.
Sprots[3] the last containing x cades	xx*s*.

T

Tallowe the c. containing v.xx xij pound	xvi*s*. viii*d*.
Thrummes the c. containing v.xx.	xx*s*.
Tin of Cornwall the c. contayning v.xx xii li.	xxxiij*s*. iiij*d*.
Tin of Devonshire the c. contayning v.xx xii pound	xxx*s*.
Tin wrought the c. containing v.xx xii pound	xlvi*s*. viij*d*.
Tips of hornes the M	x*s*.

V

Violet in grain the yarde	xiii*s*. iiij*d*.

---

[1] Ruddle, a red variety of ochre used for marking sheep and for colouring.
[2] Heather.   [3] Sprats.

W

Wheat the quarter	x*s*.
Wine look Malmesey	
Woodnets[1] the c. containing v.xx li.	vi*s*.[2]
Worsted called Norwich worsted the peece	xxx*s*.

All other goods and wares which shall be caried out of this Realme by way of merchandise and bee not mentioned among the rates for the subsidies or poundage outwards (our plesure is) shall be rated to pay custome and subsidie or poundage outwardes according unto the values and prices of the same goods mentioned in this book among the rates for the subsidie or poundage inwards.

And if there shall happen to be brought in or carried foorth in this our Realme any goods or wares liable to the pament of the said custome and subsidie or poundage, which either be omitted out of this book or be not now used to be brought in, or caried foorth, our pleasure is that in such case every our Customer or Collectour for the time beeing shall levy the said customes and subsidie or poundage according to the valure and price of such goods to be affirmed upon the othe of the Merchant in the presence of the Customer and Controuler for the time beeing until furder order shalbe taken therein by us and our Councel.

A declaration expressing the losse sustained by reason of the difference beetween the custome and subsidies of wull and Cloth, and also expressing the rate presently assessed upon Clothes.

---

[1] Wood-nuts or filberts.

[2] A mistake for 6*s*. 8*d*., which is the value given in the 1558 and 1562 Books of Rates.

The Rates for English men

Wul.

A sack of wul custome	vi*s*. viii*d*.
yeeldeth in subsidie	xxxiiii*s*. iiij*d*.

Cloth.

The custome of every short Cloth white and couloured is   xiiij*d*.

A sack of wul commonly maketh foure short Clothes, the custome wherof is,   iiii*s*. iiij*d*.[1]

And so the custome of wul in cloth is lesse then the custome and subsidie of so much wul not clothed, in every sack in short Clothes   xxxv*s*. iiii*d*.

The difference of which custome beetween wul and Cloth, is reduced to an equallitie by rating upon every short Cloth   x*s*.

Which difference between the custome of the wul and cloth considered, and the great losse sustained by us in the same, by reason that clothing is now so much increased, it is thought convenient by us, with the advice of our councell, towardes the releef of the losse, to assesse upon the clothes caryed out by the way of Merchandise some larger rate then heertofore hath been used.

And though it were reason to appoint such a Rate as might recompence the full of the losse sustained, yet upon divers considerations at this time (us and our councel mooving) wee are pleased to assesse only the rate insuing.

That is to say.

Every short cloth shipped and caried out of the Realme

---

[1] A mistake for 4*s*. 8*d*. (i.e. 4 times 1*s*. 2*d*.)

by way of merchandise by any English man shall yeeld to
us by name of custome .... vj*s*. viij*d*.

And also after the rate in all other clothes. Which exceedeth the olde custome upon every short cloth ..... v*s*. vj*d*.

And is neverthelesse under the Rate which reduceth the
Custome of Wull and Cloth to an equalitie in every short
Cloth .... iij*s*. iiij*d*.

Heer endeth the Rates outwards for english Merchants.

The Rate for Straungers.

Wul.

Every sack yeeldeth in antiqua Custome	vi*s*. viij*d*.
Item in parva custome	iij*s*. iiij*d*.
And the Subsidie	iij*l*. vj*s*. viij*d*.
Sum of all is	iij*l*. xvj*s*. viij*d*.

Cloth.

The custome and Subsidie of every short cloth white, in custome	ij*s*. ix*d*.
And the Subsidie	ij*s*.
Which in all is	iiij*s*. ix*d*.
Every short Cloth couloured in custome	ij*s*. ix*d*.
And the Subsidie	iij*s*. vj*d*.
Sum of all is	xj*s*. iiij*d*.[1]
Which amounteth in custome and Subsidie for foure short whites	xix*s*.
Foure short couloured	xxv*s*.
And so the custome and subsidie of wul put in Cloth is lesse then white clothes	lvij*s*. viij*d*.

---

[1] A mistake for vj*s*. iij*d*., which is the figure given in the 1558, 1562, and 1590 Books of Rates.

The custome and subsidie of the same wul
   unclothed, for every Sack couloured clothes   li*s*. viij*d*.
The difference of which custome is reduced to
   an equalitie, by rating upon every short
   cloth white and couloured   xix*s*. ij*d*.

   Which diversitie of the customes considered, it is thought
by us and our councel resonable for the considerations
before remembred. That every Straunger shall pay to us for
every cloth by them to be shipped or caried out of this
Realme for custome and subsidie as followeth

That is to say

For every short cloth, white and coulored the sum of
                          xiii*s*. iiij*d*.[1]
And so after the rate in all other clothes and Kerseyes.
Which exceedeth the former custome and Subsidie in every
   short cloth white,   ix*s*. ix*d*.
And the short cloth couloured   viij*s*. iiii*d*.[2]
And is neverthelesse under the rate which reduceth the
   custome and subsidie of wul and cloth to an equalitie
   in everie short cloth white and colored,   iiij*s*. viii*d*.

Rates for clothes.

   Pin whites
   Statewes
   Streits
vj Stockbridges   for a Cloth
   Cardenals
   Tavestocks

---

[1] An inexplicable mistake for 14*s*. 6*d*. The 1558 and 1562 Books of Rates have 14*s*. 6*d*., which is clearly the correct amount. The 1590 Book of Rates repeats the error of 13*s*. 4*d*.

[2] A mistake for 8*s*. 3*d*. Again the 1558 and 1562 Books of Rates give the amount correctly.

I

	Devonshire dosens	
	Penystones unfrised	
iiij	Iseland dosens	for a cloth
	Northen plaines alias Checks	

iij	Newbery whites	for a cloth
	Kerseyes of all sortes	

	Northen dosens	
	Bridge Waters	
	Florentines	
ij	Penistones frised	for a Cloth
	Devonshire dosens double	

j	Northern dosen double	for a Cloth
j	Bastard for a long Cloth which is a short Cloth and a third part of a short Cloth	

For every yarde of Cloth in grain, there is to be prooved for
    custome   ij*d.*
And for half grain   j*d.*

Finis

The end of the Rates for the Subsidie or Poundage
outwards

Scavadge[1]

A Bale	iiij*d.*
A Barrel	iiij*d.*
A Basket	vi*d.*
A Case great	viij*d.*
A Case small	iiij*d.*

---

[1] Scavage, a toll or duty on imported goods. It seems to have been paid largely by merchant strangers, but the whole question of scavage is very obscure (see Gras, pp. 33–5).

A Chest great	viij*d*.
A Chest small	iiij*d*.
A Cofer	iiij*d*.
A Fardel	viij*d*.
A Fat	viij*d*.
A Firkin	j*d*.
A Hamper	ij*d*.
A Hogshed	iiij*d*.
A Maund	viij*d*.
A Pack	xij*d*.
A Pipe	vj*d*.
A Punchion	iiij*d*.
A Trusse	iiij*d*.

A

Allrm[1] the hundred	ii*d*.
Ankers small[2] the peece	iiij*d*.
Ankers small the peece	ij*d*.
Anisseeds the bale or bag	iiij*d*.
Appuls or Peares the barrel	qr.
Ashes called Sope ashes the last	ij*d*.
Ashes called wood ashes the last	iii*d*.

B

Battery the bale	viii*d*.
Balles the tun	iiij*d*.
Bayes the sack	ii*d*.
Beer the tun	iiii*d*.
Bowstaves the c. contayning vj.xx[3]	
Box for combes the bale	iiii*d*.
Bottels the dosen	ob.

---

[1] *Sic*, for alum.   [2] A mistake for great.   [3] No duty stated.

Boords for Barrels the last thousand[1]	ii*d*.
Brasel the hundred	ii*d*.
Brimstone the barrel	ii*d*.
Buffe hides the dosen	iiij*d*.

C

Cabages the c.	ob.
Candlewick the pack	iiij*d*.
Canvas the pack	xij*d*.
Canvas called vetery Canvas the bale	ij*d*.
Carving tooles the dosen	ob.
Carpets called Turkie Carpets the peece	iiij*d*.
Cassia Fistula the sack or Chest	ii*d*.
Chayres close the peece	ob.
Chamblets the bale	xij*d*.
Chests the nest	iiij*d*.
Chests called Cipers chests the nest	viij*d*.
Clapholt or clapboard the M	vi*d*.
Coles the Chaulder	i*d*.
Combs the chest or case	ii*d*.
Copperas the but	iiij*d*.
Coralls the Mast	ii*d*.
Cork for Dyers the c.	ij*d*.
Cork for Cordwainers the dosen	ob.
Crossebow laths the c.	iiij*d*.
Cupbourds the peece	ii*d*.
Currants the but	viij*d*.

D

Dates the hogshed	iiij*d*.
Deale boordes the peece	ob.
Dry Wares the Tun	viij*d*.

---

[1] *Sic.*

F

Fethers the sack	iiij*d.*
Fethers the bag	i*d.*
Fish the hundred	iii*d.*
Fish the last	iii*d.*
Fish called Eelles of all sortes the last	iii*d.*
Fish called Herrings the last	iii*d.*
Fish called Lings the hundred	iii*d.*
Fish called Newland great the c.	iii*d.*
Fish called Newland middle the c.	ii*d.*
Fish called Newland small the c.	i*d.*
Fish called Salmon the barrel	i*d.*
Fish called Staple Fish the c.	iij*d.*
Figges the great peece	ob.
Figges every iij quarters of a c.	ob.
Flax the pack	xii*d*
Flax the c bundles made	vi*d.*
Flax the hundred	i*d.*
Flaunders tile the thousand	ii*d.*

G

Garlick the c bunches	i*d.*
Galles the sack or bale	ii*d.*
Glasse the case	ii*d.*
Glasse the Chest	iiij*d.*
Grayn for Dyers the C	ij*d.*

H

Harp strings the box	i*d.*
Hemp the hundred	i*d.*
Hemp the sack	iiij*d.*
Hemp called Cullen hemp the bale	ii*d.*
Hops the pocket	i*d.*

| Hops the poke | ii*d.* |
| Hops the sack | iiij*d.* |

I

Imagery the box	ob.
Iron the tun	v*s.*
Iron pointels the dosen	i*d.*
Iron Kettle bands the c.	i*d.*

L

Latten the barrel	iiij*d.*
Lawn the peece	ii*d.*
Lead the Fodder	iiii*d.*
Lemmons the thousand	ii*d.*
Licoris the bale	ii*d.*
Litmouse the sack	iiij*d.*
Linnen cloth called Holland cloth the chest	xii*d.*
Lockeram the peece	ob.

M

Madder the bale	viii*d.*
Madder the hogshed	vi*d.*
Madder called Mul madder the bale	ob.
Marmelade the barrel	ii*d.*
Masts great the peece	iiii*d.*
Masts small the peece	ii*d.*
Minsters the roule	iiij*d.*
Musterd seed the pipe	ii*d.*

N

Nayles of all sorts the barrel	iiij*d.*
Nuts called small nuts the barrel	i*d.*
Nuts called small nuts the pipe	iiii*d.*

Nuts called small nuts the tun	viij*d*.
Nuts called wall nuts the barrel	i*d*.
Nuts called wall nuts the pipe or puncheon[1]	

O

Onions the barrel	qr.
Onions the c bunches	i*d*.
Onion seed the sack	ij*d*.
Orenges the M	ii*d*.
Ores the hundred	iiii*d*.
Orchall made the last	iiii*d*.
Orchall the sack	iiij*d*.
Osmunds the last	iij*d*.
Ozenbridges the role	iiij*d*.
Oyle the barrel	iiij*d*.
Oyle the pipe or but	xvi*d*.
Oyle the tun	ii*s*. viii*d*.
Oyle called Trane Oyle the barrell	iiii*d*.

P

Paper the bale	iiij*d*.
Paper the pack	xij*d*.
Paper called brown Paper the c bundels	iiij*d*.
Paving tile the M	i*d*.
Paving Tile painted the c.	i*d*.
Peltrie the sack	vi*d*.
Pepper the bag[2]	
Pepper the c pound	iiij*d*.
Pewter the hogshed	viij*d*.
Pitch and Tar the last	iij*d*.
Pipes the bale	ij*d*.

---

[1] No duty stated.   [2] Ibid.

Plate white or black the barrel	ii*d*.
Plaster of Paris the mount	ob.
Pomegranats the M	iiij*d*.
Pots called Cruses the maund	iij*d*.
Pots called Galley pots the c.	i*d*.
Pots with covers or without covers the c.	i*d*.
Prunes the pipe or barrel	iiij*d*.

Q

Quailes the Cage	ij*d*.

R

Raysins the peece	ob.
Rice the bag[1]	
Rosen the peece	ob.
Ropes called bast Ropes the c.	i*d*.
Ropes called Cables the hundred	i*d*.

S

Salt the way	ij*d*.
Saffron the pound	ob.
Sheres for Sheremen the paire	ob.
Silk called Cullen Silk the pound	ob.
Silk called long silk the pound	ob.
Silk called short Silk the pound	qr.
Silks the chest	xij*d*.
Sope the c. or barrel	i*d*.
Sope the last	xij*d*.
Sope white the case	iii*d*.
Sope white the hundred	i*d*.
Skinnes called Beavers the Bag	ij*d*.
Skinnes called Beavers the basket	vi*d*.

---

[1] No duty stated.

Skinnes called Beavers the role	i*d*.
Skinnes called Budge, tawed or untawed the hundred	ij*d*.
Skinnes called Cordwain skinnes the dosen	ii*d*.
Skinnes called Cunny skinnes the thousand	ii*d*.
Skinnes called Lambskinnes the hundred	ij*d*.
Skinnes called Portingale skinnes the dosen	ij*d*.
Skinnes called Sables course the timber	vj*d*.
Skinnes called Sables fine the timber	xii*d*.
Skinnes called Spanish skinnes the dosen	ii*d*.
Sparres or Rafters[1] the c.	i*d*.
Splinters the sack	iiij*d*.
Steel the barrel	iiij*d*.
Stones called Cane stones the tun	i*d*.
Stones called Dog stones the last	iiii*d*.
Stones called Mil stones great the peece	viij*d*.
Stones called Mil stones small the peece	iiii*d*.
Stones called Quern stones the last	iiii*d*.
Stones called Alablaster the lode	iiii*d*.
Sturgeon the barrel	ij*d*.
Succade the barrel	i*d*.
Sugar or sugar Candie the chest	iiii*d*.
Swoord blades the dosen	i*d*.

T

Tankerds or Cannes the shock	i*d*.
Tazels the Kief	qr.
Tazels the Pipe	iiii*d*.
Tin Glasse the hundred	i*d*.
Tin the block	iiij*d*.
Tin the hundred	i*d*.
Tunny the barrel	iiii*d*.

---

[1] The 1590 Book of Rates has 'Sparres for Rafters'.

Trayes the shock	ii*d*.
Treacle the barrel	iiii*d*.
Thred the bale	iiij*d*.

V

Vinager the pipe	ob.

W

Wax the hundred	ij*d*.
Wainscot the C	iiij*d*.
Wire the barrel	iiij*d*.
Wire called Latten wire the ring	ob.
Wine the tun	ij*d*.
Wod the ballet	ij*d*.
Wul called Cotten wul the Sack	viij*d*.
Wul called Estridge wul the Sack	viij*d*.
Wul called Hatters wul the Sack	iiij*d*.
Wul the sack	iiij*d*.

Finis

The true difference of Measures and Weights

The Flemish elle and the English yarde

One Flemish elle maketh iij quarters of an English yarde

v	make iii yards and iii quarters
x	make vii yards and di.
xx	make xv yardes
j hundred	make seventie v yardes
j thousand	make vii hundred l yardes

The Flemish elle and the English elle

v	make iii elles
x	make vi elles
xx	make xii elles
i hundred	make lx elles
i thousand	make vi.c elles

The Braces of Italie and the English yarde

v Braces	make three yardes
x	make vi yardes
xv	make ix yardes
xx	make xii yardes
i hundred	make lx yardes
i thousand	make vi.c yardes

The Braces of Italy and the english elle

v	make ii elles and ii quarters of a yarde
x	make iiii elles iiii quarters
xv	make vii elles one quarter
xx	make ix elles three quarters
C	make xlviii elles
M	make iiiiC viii elles

The Pannes of Jean and the English yarde

iiij	make i yarde
xii	make iii yardes
xx	make v yardes
C	make xxv yardes
M	make iiC l yardes

The Vares of Spaine and the English yarde

iiii and di.	make iiii yardes
ix	make viii yardes
xviii	make xvi yardes
xxxvi	make xxxii yardes
lxxii	make lxiiii yardes
C	make lxxxviii yardes and viii.ix parts
M	make 888 yards and viii.ix partes

Spruce weights and English Weights

viii Lispound	make a c pound
xxviii Lispound	make i Ship pound
i Ship pound	make two c.l. pounds
xx Ship pound	make vM pounds

What number of all kinde of dry French wares make a Tun

Wares	Hogshed
Wol cardes	Fiftie dosen
playing cardes	xii groce and a di.
Canvas	vi hundred l elles
Combes	iCxxv groce
Beades	lx groce
Glasse	Five Cases
Paper	Fiftie Reames
Boultel	Ten Bales
Dornix	One M Elles
Buckerams	Twelve dosen and di.
Paris thred	Two C.l. Bales
Rains boultel	xxv dosen
Poldavis or Oulderons	xxv peeces
Wod	Five Ballets
Rosen	Five C weight

Wares	Hogshed
Lockeram or Dowlas	xiii dosen peeces
Quilts	Fiftie quilts

Pipe[1]	Tun[1]
a C dosen	Two C dosen
xxv groce	Fiftie groce
One M iii.c elles	iiM vi.c elles
Two c.l. groce	Five C groce
Cxx groce	two c.xl. groce
Ten cases	Twentie cases
A C Remes	two C Remes
Twentie bales	Fortie bales
Two M elles	Foure M elles
Twentie v dosen	Fiftie Dosen
Five C buts	One M Buts
Fiftie dosen	One C dosen
Fiftie peeces	One C peeces
Ten ballets	twentie ballets
One M weight	two M weight
Twentie vi dosen peeces	Fiftie dosen[2] peeces
One C Quilts	Two C quilts

A true discription of Troy weight and Haberdepoiz weight.

First xi[3] Wheate cornes of the midst of the eare of white Wheat beeing faire, full and dry, doo make one peny weight.

Item lx of those pence doo make an unce weight. And xii

---

[1] These measures refer to the same list of wares, i.e. Woolcards, etc. They are printed in this way in the original, where the page is too narrow to take four columns, which would be the more convenient form.

[2] Presumably this should be 52 dozen, as the tun was obviously twice the pipe.

[3] The 1590 Book of Rates has 12 wheat corns.

of those unces make a pound of Troy weight, And a pound of Troy maketh three pound of our silver coine.

But the Goldesmiths and the bakers doo recken xxxii of the said wheat cornes to a peny weight, as it hath been in use a long time since.

Of Haberdepoiz weight,

Of Troy weight xiiii unces and a half and half quarter doo make a pound called Haberdepoiz weight.

And by this weight men buy and sell the moste part of merchandize in this Realme, as Lead, Tinne, Iron, copper, Steele, Wax, Wod, Silk, thred, Flax, hemp, Ropes, Tallow and all manner of such other merchantize.

And by the difference of this weight, beeing truely reduced into the weights in other countries a man may knowe how to make his reconing the better

Finis

Imprinted at
London at the long Shop adjoyning
unto S. Mildreds Church in the Pultrie
by John Allde.

INDEX OF COMMODITIES

K

Gentian, 28
Ghentish cloth, 28
Gimlets, 28
Ginger, xl, 28; green, 28
Gingerbread, xli
Girdles, l, 28, 65
Girth web, 28
Gitterns, *see* Citherns
Glass, 28, 77, 84
Glasses, xxxv, 23, 29
Glovers clippings, 67
Gloves, 29
Glue, 29
Goatskins, 29
Gold of Bruges, 29
Gold foil, 29; papers, 29; skins, 29
Goose quills, 67
Grain, 77; of Portugal, 29; of Seville, 29
Grain powder, 29
Grains, 30
Grana pene, 30
Gratia dei, 63
Gray, 30; skins, 30
Great raisins, xxxviii, xlii, 30
Grogram, 30; camlets, 30
Gull-fish, 30
Gum ammoniac, 30; arabic, 30; edere, 30; elemi, 30; imperii, 30; opopanax, 30; serapinum, xxxiii, 30; tragacanth, 30
Gunpowder, 31
Guns, 31

Haddocks, 31
Halberts, 31
Halstred (cloth), 32
Hammers, 31 n. 3
Hampers, 31
Handkerchiefs, 31
Handovers (cloth), 31
Hanging locks, 31
Harmodacus, *see* Hermodactyl
Harnesdale cloth, 31
Harness, 31; nails, 31
Harp strings, 31–2, 77
Hasbrough cloth, 32
Hassors (cloth), 32
Hat bands, 32

Hatchets, 6
Hats, 7, 32
Hawks, xxviii, 32; hoods, 32
Heath, for brushes, xxxv, 33; red, 69
Hedlack (cloth), 32
Hemp, xl, xlii, 32–3, 77, 86
Henigo cloth, 33
Hermodactyl, 31
Hernshewes, *see* Heronsews
Heronsews, 33
Herrings, 33
Hides, xxxix
Hilts, l; for daggers, 33; for swords, 33
Hinderlands (cloth), 33
Holland cloth, xxxviii, xlii, xlvi, 33, 78
Honey, 33
Hook ends, 33
Hooks, 33
Hoops for barrels, 33
Hops, 33, 77–8
Horns, 67; for blowing, 33; for lanterns, 33
Horse collars, 67; combs, 33; tails, 67
Hose, 33, 67
Hour glasses, 33–4
Huss skins, 34
Hypocistis, 35

Imagery, 78
Imperlings, 34
Indigo, xxxix, xlvi–xlvii
Ink, 34; horns, 34, 46
Inkle, 34–5
Ipocestes, *see* Hypocistis
Ireos, 24
Iron, xxiv, xxxviii, xlv, 35, 67, 78, 86; backs, 35; bands, 35, 78; chests, 35; plates, 23; pointels, 78; pots, xxxv, 35; wire, 35
Isingham cloth, 35
Isinglass, xxviii, 36
Ivory, 36

Jasper stones, 34
Javelin heads, 34; staves, 34
Jennets, 34
Jet, xxii, 34